POSERS, FAKERS, & WANNABES

(UNMASKING THE REAL YOU)

Go Ahead:

TH1NK: *about God*

about life

about others

Faith isn't just an act; it's something you live—something huge and sometimes unimaginable. By getting into the real issues in your life, TH1NK books open opportunities to talk honestly about your faith, your relationship with God and others, as well as all the things life throws at you.

Don't let other people th1nk for you . . .

TH1NK for yourself.

www.th1nkbooks.com

POSERS, FAKERS, & WANNABES

(UNMASKING THE REAL YOU)

BRENNAN MANNING
AND JIM HANCOCK

TH1NK Books
an imprint of NavPress®

NAVPRESS
P.O. Box 35001
Colorado Springs, CO 80935

The Navigators is an international Christian organization. Our mission is to reach, disciple, and equip people to know Christ and to make Him known through successive generations. We envision multitudes of diverse people in the United States and every other nation who have a passionate love for Christ, live a lifestyle of sharing Christ's love, and multiply spiritual laborers among those without Christ.

NavPress is the publishing ministry of The Navigators. NavPress publications help believers learn biblical truth and apply what they learn to their lives and ministries. Our mission is to stimulate spiritual formation among our readers.

NAVPRESS, BRINGING TRUTH TO LIFE, and the NAVPRESS logo are registered trademarks of NavPress. Absence of ® in connection with marks of NavPress or other parties does not indicate an absence of registration of those marks.

ISBN 1-57683-465-4

Cover and interior design by BURNKIT (www.burnkit.com)

Creative Team: Jay Howver, Karen Lee-Thorp, Darla Hightower, Glynese Northam

Some of the anecdotal illustrations in this book are true to life and are included with the permission of the persons involved. All other illustrations are composites of real situations, and any resemblance to people living or dead is coincidental.

This book incorporates content originally included in *Abba's Child*, copyright 1994 by Brennan Manning, published by NavPress.

Manning, Brennan.
  Posers, fakers, and wannabes : unmasking the real you / Brennan
Manning with Jim Hancock.
     p. cm.
Summary: Provides insight into behaving as a child of God, knowing that
He loves each person's true self, not the "poser" that maintains the
appearance that life is not out of control and in need of God's help.
Includes bibliographical references.
  ISBN 1-57683-465-4
  1. Teenagers--Religious life. 2. Teenagers--Conduct of life. [1.
Christian life. 2. Conduct of life. 3. Self-acceptance.] I. Hancock,
Jim, 1952- II. Title.
  BV4531.3 .M36 2003
  248.8'3--dc22
                                    2003011972

Printed in Canada

2 3 4 5 6 7 8 9 10 / 08 07 06 05 04

FOR A FREE CATALOG OF
NAVPRESS BOOKS & BIBLE STUDIES,
CALL 1-800-366-7788 (USA)
OR 1-416-499-4615 (CANADA)

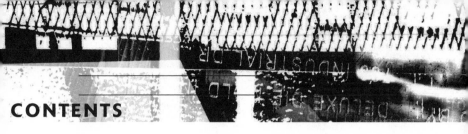

CONTENTS

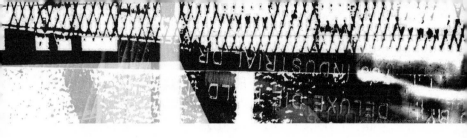

WHY THIS BOOK?

to be nobody but yourself in a world which is doing its best day and night to make you everybody else, means to fight the hardest battle which any human being can fight, and never stop fighting.
—e.e. cummings

A NOTE FROM BRENNAN MANNING

In 1994 I published a book called *Abba's Child*, with a chapter titled "The Impostor." That chapter got more attention than all the others combined. For a lot of readers, "The Impostor" is what *Abba's Child* is about. I'm not surprised.

The Impostor keeps showing up in my life in new and sinister disguises. The slick impersonator of my true self stalks me day and night. These days he takes advantage of my "senior moments," blocking any memory of whether I gobbled my antidepressant and vitamin pills this morning.

This cunning poseur (that's poser, in American English) exploits my temporary amnesia to make me forget that everything I am is grace. Everything. Even the grace to grasp grace is grace. Instead of being stunned by the extravagance of God's love, many days I just expect it. In place of heartfelt gratitude for the sheer, unearned abundance of God's gifts, I'm often gripped by an arrogant satisfaction in my accomplishments and the false security of spiritual superiority.

The Impostor is baffling, sneaky, and seductive. At the same time he tempts me with self-satisfaction, he also undermines my truest self, my identity as Abba's beloved child. (*Abba* is a rather intimate Aramaic word for *father*, roughly equivalent to the English words *daddy* or *papa*. Jesus shocked first-century religious leaders by addressing the Creator as *Daddy*—*Abba*. More on that later.) The Imposter tries to convince me that, no matter what God says, *Abba's Child* is a false identity, completely out of my reach. The Impostor wants me to believe my only hope is to forsake my true self and become, as e.e. cummings put it, "everybody else."

If it weren't me, I would say it was a fascinating struggle. My greatest difficulty in recent years has been bringing The Impostor—*The Poser*—into the presence of Jesus instead of trying to whip him into shape on my own. But it is me, and there's nothing fascinating about it. I want to beat The Poser into submission. I want to win this war with myself. Bitter irony. Instead of surrendering my self-centeredness to Christ, I try to beat it to death. Then I get discouraged and decide my alleged spiritual life is just self-deception and fantasy.

I have a history with this behavior. When I was twenty-three years old I was a novice in the Franciscan Order in Washington, D.C. The order practiced an ancient spiritual discipline on the Friday nights of Lent. A priest stood flat-footed beside the stairwell on the first floor, slowly and loudly reciting Psalm 51 in Latin. *Miserere me, Domine, secundum misericordiam, tuam* . . . while the rest of us entered our tiny rooms on the second floor, each clutching a twelve-inch, noose-shaped instrument of torture; it was coiled telephone wire. Following this ancient tradition, for the duration of the psalm we whipped our backs and buttocks to extinguish the fires of lust. That first Friday night, I flailed away with such reckless abandon that I raised blood blisters on my back.

The next day in the shower room, a priest took one look at my bludgeoned body and reported my condition to the novice master, who reprimanded me for going overboard. Well of course I went overboard. I was trying desperately to make myself pleasing to God.

This was not the case with Brother Dismas, who lived in the cell next to mine. I was listening as he scourged himself so savagely I feared for both his health and his sanity—so savagely that I risked a peek through his cracked door. There he sat with a bemused smile and a cigarette in his left hand. It was the wall he was whacking, not his own body, *thwack, thwack, thwack.* My response? I pitied the poor wretch and returned to my cell with an insufferable sense of spiritual superiority.

I don't much recommend his approach or mine.

///

Writing *Abba's Child* was a profound spiritual experience for me, and reading it, I'm told, has been a profound experience for people around the world. *Abba's Child* has been translated into languages I don't speak because, apparently, people in other cultures—Spanish, French, German—get it if it's in their native tongues. It excites me to know I've somehow communicated truth that crosses cultural divides.

Now I've come to recognize an English dialect I don't speak, at least not well. It's the language of pop culture, the dialect of the young. So, the veteran youth worker Jim Hancock and I are translating *Abba's Child* for emerging generations of readers. We're calling this translation *Posers, Fakers, and Wannabes.*

I'm praying this new book will go places I can't go to reach people whose hearts I know, even if we don't exactly speak the same language.

I join my old and now retired spiritual director, Larry Hein, who wrote this blessing:

> *May all your expectations be frustrated, may all your plans be thwarted, may all your desires be withered into nothingness, that you may experience the powerlessness and poverty of a child and sing and dance in the love of God who is Father, Son, and Spirit. And today on planet Earth, may you experience the wonder and beauty of yourself as Abba's child and temple of the Holy Spirit through Jesus Christ our Lord.*

—BRENNAN MANNING

A NOTE FROM JIM HANCOCK

Brennan and I came to *Posers, Fakers, and Wannabes* by different roads. I'm an old Presbyterian youth worker, the adult child of a Southern Baptist preacher's family, a recovering fundamentalist.

I first took advice from The Poser when I was faking my way through junior high school. I wanted to fit in. I was afraid of being left out. The Poser helped me appear better than I was (or worse if worse was better). He helped me conceal the truth from people I thought might judge me as harshly as *I* judged me. I kept taking his advice because, mostly, it worked.

The Poser is *the man of a thousand faces.* He taught me how to construct a mask for any occasion from whatever I found lying around. With my musical friends I was all about whatever music they liked. For my jock friends I was brooding and barely verbal. When I got with smart kids I bluffed my way through by recalling trivia and making up stuff (wait a minute . . . I think I still do that!). With The Poser's help I managed to hold my own into high school, but it was hard, exhausting work. I went to church (spiritual face), I hung out with friends (wise guy face), I went out a little (sincere face). So many disguises, so little real fun, playing all those roles without knowing who *I* was. Or if I was anyone at all.

I was on an impossible quest, searching for my identity in the eyes of other people. Some of them I admired too much because, as my friend Michael Yaconelli says, I judged what I knew about me by what I *didn't* know about them. I feared some of them because they were power brokers who could make or break a person's social status on a whim. And there were a few who were simply fascinating because, as far as I could see, they didn't care what the rest of us thought about them—didn't care if we thought of them at all.

I played to all of them. I didn't know what else to do.

If I knew then what I know now I could have relaxed; I could have treated myself more generously; I could have stopped trying to improve on the truth.

///

I was at summer camp when I realized I might not have what it takes to be happy, let alone good. As far as I knew, my sophomore year was as good as life gets, and I hated it. I stared cold sober at the best year of my life and said right out loud, *I've screwed up everything I ever tried.* I was tired of being afraid. I was tired of being alone. I was tired of being a fake.

So, for the first time in my life, I surrendered. I gave in to the hope that God might do for me what I could not do for myself. I was the prodigal son, coming back to ask my old man for a job on the farm. I was Pinocchio returning home—having made an ass of myself, my nose a mile long from all the lies—hoping like crazy Gepetto could (and would) make me a real boy.

And you know what? He did. Eleventh grade was a blur of happy feelings and good times. And I really was becoming a better person—treating people better and taking responsibility. What's more, I felt more authentically spiritual than ever; sometimes I woke up in the middle of the night to pray and write in my notebook and then drift off happily to sleep again. It was wonderful.

Until I started faking it.

"Started faking it" sounds too abrupt, as if one day it was real and the next day it wasn't. Here's how The Poser snuck up on me: My week at summer camp was so far beyond anything I'd experienced before, even though I grew up going to church, that I wasn't sure I knew anyone back home who was a Christian like I had become a Christian. That was a sincere point of view; it wasn't arrogance. Not yet.

I asked around my hometown and met someone who claimed to be a Christian like me. He seemed like a good guy and we agreed to study the Bible together. We added another guy and another, then a couple more, and we had ourselves a small group. It was good! I'd never studied the Bible on my own, and what we were up to seemed alive and real in a way nothing ever had.

It wasn't long before some good-hearted adults started coaching me in a three-step outline for telling people about my new faith:

> I. *My Life Before I Met Christ*
> II. *How I Met Christ*
> III. *My Life After Meeting Christ*

What could be simpler, clearer, more honest and direct than that?

Well, for one thing, the truth about step III: My Life After Meeting Christ. Six months down the road I would certainly have gotten a "Much Improved" on my spiritual report card, but it just as certainly wouldn't have been (nor is it today) an "A+." Progress? Yes. Perfection? You gotta be kiddin'.

That's when The Poser checked back in. He knew and pointed out in some detail how incomplete my life-change was. Since I was already on record with my friends and family that EVERYTHING HAD CHANGED! and it was too late to turn back, he suggested I should maybe dance around the actual facts of my experience (just a little) to keep people from being confused and disappointed.

He suggested I should maybe dance around the actual facts of my experience (just a little) to keep people from being confused and disappointed.

And that's what I did for . . . I don't know . . . twenty years, give or take. I was a peer leader, then a card-carrying youth pastor in those twenty years. I became a husband and a father. I spoke at retreats and created resources for youth workers. And I'm proud to report, with the competent assistance of The Poser, I made it work, mostly. I've been advised by The Poser to inform you that, unlike Brennan, who will admit he's an alcoholic, sober by the grace of God, I've never been drunk, never smoked, never slept with anyone but my wife, never cheated on a test, never shoplifted. You can see my record is quite clear, right?

Uh . . . not exactly. All those statements are factually correct without being true at all because I've never been tempted to do those things.

I haven't been drunk or smoked, but I've been dangerously overweight because I'm constantly tempted to binge when I'm in pain or in doubt or angry or sad—or, for that matter, happy. Food is my drug of choice (legal, cheap, and readily available!). I've never slept with anyone but my wife, but I've still been lusty and sexually compulsive, and I'm tempted every day to return to that behavior. I've never cheated on a test, but I exaggerate and I'm constantly tempted to lie so people will think better of me (and I know how to make this work because I've done it so often). I've never shoplifted, but I've used my credit cards to spend thousands of dollars on things I didn't need because what I was really purchasing was the emotional rush of buying stuff to ease whatever pain or lack I felt at the time (instead of surrendering that pain to Jesus). And I'm still tempted to do that, just about every day. I don't think I get any points for what I haven't done because, sooner or later, I've done everything I've been seriously tempted to do.

Right now The Poser is very unhappy with me. He doesn't like it when I talk this way. He's still afraid of the truth, afraid you'll put down the book and ask for your money back because why in the world would anybody read a book by a sober drunk and a barely recovering fake?

Brennan and I have agreed to tell The Poser to mind his own business while we set the record straight on a few things. Because we're sick of being posers, fakers, and wannabes and, more than anything, we want to live like what we most truly are—Abba's children.

III

To keep things simple, in this book the personal pronoun "I" refers to Brennan (if "I" ever means Jim, we'll let you know). The collective pronoun "we" refers to us and all our fellow posers, fakers, and wannabes—we know who we are. . . .

Here's hoping all this is as useful to you as it is to us. Let us know what you think.

—JIM HANCOCK

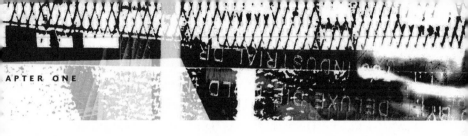

COME OUT, COME OUT,
WHEREVER YOU ARE

Night. Ruller lies awake, listening to his parents in the next room.

"Ruller's an unusual one," his father says. "Why does he always play by himself?"

"How am I to know?" Ruller's mother says in the dark.

Ruller is Flannery O'Connor's creation; a small-town kid waking up to the world.

Day. Ruller chases a wild and wounded turkey through the woods. *Oh, if only I can catch it,* he thinks, and by golly he *will* catch it if he has to run right out of the state to do it. Ruller sees himself marching through the front door, the turkey slung over his shoulder and the whole family, amazed, shouting, "Look at Ruller with that wild turkey! Ruller, where did you get that turkey?"

"Oh, I caught it in the woods. Maybe you would like me to catch you one sometime."

But catching the wounded bird is harder than he thought. Another idea occurs to Ruller: "God will probably make me chase that damn turkey all afternoon for nothing." He knows he shouldn't think that way about God—but it's how he feels. And who can blame him if that's the way he feels?

Ruller trips and falls and lies there in the dirt, wondering if he's unusual.

Suddenly the chase is over. The turkey drops dead from the gun-shot wound that crippled it. Ruller hoists the bird on his shoulders and starts a victory march toward home, right down the center of town. He remembers his thoughts about God before he got the turkey. They were pretty bad, he guesses. This is probably God getting his attention, stopping him before he goes wild like his brother. "Thank You, God," he says. "You were mighty generous."

He thinks maybe the turkey is a sign. Maybe God wants him to be a preacher. Ruller wants to do something for God. If he saw a poor person on the street today, he would give away his dime. It's the only dime he has, but he thinks he would give it to that person for God.

Ruller is walking through town now, and people are knocked out by the size of his turkey. Men and women stare. A group of country kids trail behind him. "How much do you think it weighs?" a man asks.

"At least ten pounds," Ruller says.

"How long did you chase it?"

"About an hour," Ruller replies.

"That's really amazing."

But Ruller doesn't have time for chitchat. He can't wait to hear what they say when he gets that turkey home.

He wishes he would see someone begging. He would, for sure, give them his only dime. "Lord, send me a beggar. Send me one before I get home." And he knows for a fact God will send him a beggar because he is an unusual child.

"Please, one right now," Ruller prays—and the minute he says it, an old beggar woman heads straight toward him. His heart stomps up and down in his chest. He springs at the woman, shouting, "Here, here!" He thrusts the dime into her hand, then dashes off without looking back.

Slowly his heart calms and he feels something new—like being happy and embarrassed at the same time. Ruller is flying—him and God's turkey.

This is when Ruller notices the country kids shuffling up behind him. He turns generously to face them: "Y'all wanna see this turkey?"

They stare. "I chased it dead. See, it's been shot under the wing."

"Lemme see it," one of the boys says. Then, incredibly, the boy slings the bird over his own shoulder, hitting Ruller in the face with it as he turns. And that's that. The boys saunter away with God's turkey.

They are a block away before Ruller even moves. As they disappear in the falling dark, Ruller creeps toward home, breaking into a run. And Flannery O'Connor ends Ruller's remarkable story with the words: "He ran faster and faster, and as he turned up the road to his house, his heart was running as fast as his legs and he was certain that Something Awful was tearing behind him with its arms rigid and its fingers ready to clutch."[1]

Something Awful.

FEAR

"What comes into our minds when we think about God is the most important thing about us."[2] A. W. Tozer wrote that, talking about how people project their opinions about God onto the world. He was asking those of us who believe in God—which is most of us—what God it is we believe in. Good question.

A lot of us think what Ruller thinks about God. The God we believe in is Someone who gives a turkey with one hand and takes it away with the other. The giving is a sign that God cares about us. We feel close to God when we get what we want, and it makes us feel generous too. So everybody wins, right?

The story is different when we lose a turkey—it's a clear sign of rejection. We look for a reason. *Where did I go wrong? Why is God angry with me? Is God trying to teach me something?*

Most of us never say it out loud or even dare think it for long, but losing a turkey makes us think God is unpredictable, bad-tempered, mean, unfair. Those thoughts drive us away from God, deeper into ourselves. Now God is a bookkeeper counting every false step, every mistake, every screwup, and holding them against us. God is a grudge-holder who gets back at us by snatching family, friendship, health, money, contentment, success, and joy right out of our hands.

Losing a turkey makes us think God is unpredictable, bad-tempered, mean, unfair.

But then we think, *Who can blame God? Seriously. Just look at me— LOOK AT ME! I'm a mess. I never should have gotten the turkey to begin with. If it hadn't dropped dead in front of me, I wouldn't have.*

So we project onto God our worst attitudes and feelings about ourselves. As someone famously remarked, "God made us in his own image and we have more than returned the compliment." If we feel hatred for ourselves, it only makes sense that God hates us. Right?

No, not so much.

It's no good assuming God feels about us the way we feel about our-selves—unless we love ourselves intensely and freely with complete wisdom and never-ending compassion. If the Christian story is true, the God who shows his love for us everywhere, in everything, expresses that love completely and finally in what Jesus did for us. Deal done—can't add to, can't subtract from it. Any questions?

Well, yes. As a matter of fact we have quite a few questions. These declarations about God's love are a lot easier for Christians to say—especially to others—than to actually believe. Julian of Norwich put her finger right on the bruise when she wrote: "Some of us believe that God is almighty and can do everything; and that he is all-wise and may do everything; but that he is all-love and will do everything—there we draw back. As I see it, this ignorance is the greatest of all hindrances to God's lovers."[3] Where do we think we are going when we draw back from God?

The tiny gods we worship when we draw back from the true God are idols we've made to look just like us. It takes a profound conversion to accept that God is relentlessly tender and compassionate toward us just as we are—and not in spite of our sins and faults, but in them and through them. As Anne Lamott sees it, "The secret is that God loves us *exactly* the way we are *and* that he loves us too much to let us stay like this, and I'm just trying to trust that."[4] She makes two things plain here: God won't stop working on us until the job is complete AND God doesn't hold back his love because there is evil in us. Not now, not ever.

One night a friend asked his handicapped son, "Daniel, when you see Jesus looking at you, what do you see in his eyes?"

After a long pause, the boy replied, "His eyes are filled with tears, Dad."

Now it was his father's turn to hesitate: "Why, Dan?"

An even longer pause. "Because he is sad."

"And why is he sad?"

Daniel stared at the floor. When he looked up, his eyes were rimmed with tears. "Because I'm afraid."

Wow. It's not supposed to be like that. God never meant for us to be afraid. "There is no room in love for fear," John says. "Well-formed love banishes fear. Since fear is crippling, a fearful life—fear of death, fear of judgment—is one not yet fully formed in love."[5] It breaks God's heart that we are afraid of him, afraid of life, afraid of each other, afraid of ourselves.

So we do everything in our power to remain self-absorbed, self-sufficient, self-satisfied. "Better the devil you know," the saying goes, "than the angel you don't."

It breaks God's heart that we run *from* him instead of *to* him when we fail.

It breaks God's heart that we run from *him* instead of to *him* when we fail.

HATE

For an alcoholic, a "slip" is a terrifying experience. The physical and mental obsession with booze comes like a flash flood in a place everyone thought was high and dry. When the drunk sobers up, he or she is devastated.

This is not academic. I'm an alcoholic. My life was ruined by alcohol abuse and restored by the relentless tenderness of Jesus. When I relapsed, I faced two (and only two) options: surrender again to guilt, fear, depression, and maybe death by alcohol; or rush back to the arms of my heavenly Father.

Here's the thing: It's no trick to feel loved by God with our lives together and our support systems in place. Self-acceptance comes easy when we feel strong.

But what about when we lose control? What about when we do wrong or fail to do right, when our dreams shatter, when the people we love don't trust us, when we disappoint even ourselves? What about when we are no better than the people we always looked down on? What then?

Ask someone who's just gone through a breakup, a lost friendship, or her parents' divorce. Does she have it together now? Does she feel secure? Worthy? Does she feel like a dearly loved child of Abba, or did she lose the sense of God's love when she lost control? Does she experience God's love when everything feels broken or only when things are *good*—only when *she's good?*

God is not shocked when we fail. No more than a mother is stunned by her toddler's stumbling and falling and getting into fixes he can't get out of. Julian of Norwich wrote, "Our Lord does not want his servants to despair," however often and however hard we tumble because, "our falling does not hinder him in loving us."[6]

That's hard to believe. People like us are skeptical about that kind of thing. We believe there must be a catch. And if it's difficult to get our minds around, it's even harder to truly accept in our deepest hearts. We're so timid (or is it proud?) we can hardly bring ourselves to ask for the mercy we need. Not because we hate God and not because God hates us, but because we hate ourselves.

SAFETY

Get this if you don't get anything else: The spiritual life begins with accepting God's wholehearted love for our wounded, broken, surly, frightened, sorry selves. There is no other starting point.

God calls us every one to come out of hiding. God calls us back from wherever we went running for our lives, calls us back home. God is the love-crazed father at the window, waiting for a lost boy to come to his senses, gazing down the road for a sign of his return, now running to meet and embrace and more-than-half-carry his kid the last mile so they can start all over, as if nothing bad ever happened between them, as if the party he intends to throw that very night is the celebration of his child's birth.

It's always been this way. Adam and Eve were ashamed when they disobeyed God, so they hid themselves. And one way or another, they've been role models ever since. Why? Because we hate being seen for what we truly are, which has almost nothing to do with being as bad as we could possibly be and almost everything to do with failing to be all we could be and should be—what we aspire and maybe even pretend to be.

We know the truth—or at least much of the truth—about ourselves, and it's not all that pretty. Our way of dealing with the ugliness is mainly misdirection: Hey, look how ugly *that* guy is! Look at all the things I *don't* do! Our solution is faking it, taking cover when we lose our nerve—hiding out. Which is no solution at all.

Simon Tugwell wrote:

> *We hide what we know or feel ourselves to be (which we assume*
> *to be unacceptable and unlovable) behind some kind of appear-*
> *ance which we hope will be more pleasing. We hide behind*
> *pretty faces which we put on for the benefit of our public. And*
> *in time we may even come to forget that we are hiding, and*
> *think that our assumed pretty face is what we really look like.*[7]

Well, surprise! Whether anyone bothered to tell us this before, and whether we like it or not, God loves who we really and truly are. God calls us, as God has called everyone since Adam and Eve, to come out of hiding just as we really and truly are. No amount of spiritual cosmetology can make us more presentable to God—God buys us in an *As-Is* condition and says, "I've been looking for you! I have just the place for you!"

If what God says is the truest thing about us, then it makes sense to follow him and accept our *As-Is* condition as the starting point. Thomas Merton said, "The reason we never enter into the deepest reality of our relationship with God is that we so seldom acknowledge our utter nothingness before him."[8] If we confess the truth about ourselves, there's every reason to fear God will say, "Yeah, that's right; and *another* thing . . ." and we're fairly sure there will always be another thing. We are like people afraid to tell the doctor where we really hurt because we fear we may be sicker than we think.

We *are* sicker than we think. We're dying and, crazily, running from the healer because we're ashamed, because we hate ourselves for all we are and all we're not.

God, who spoke us into existence, speaks to us now: "Come out of self-hatred into my love. Come to me *now*," he says. "Forget about yourself. Accept who I long to be for you, who *I am* for you—your Rescuer—endlessly loving, forever patient, unbearably forgiving. Stop projecting your sick feelings onto me. You are a broken flower—I will not crush you—a flickering candle—I will not extinguish you. For once and forever, relax: *of all places, you are safe with me.*"

For once and forever, relax: of all places, you are safe with me.

REJECTION

One of the most shocking contradictions among Christian people is the intense dislike we have for ourselves. We are more disgusted and far less tolerant about our own weakness than we would dream of being with someone else. David Seamands saw it like this:

> *Satan's greatest psychological weapon is a gut level feeling of inferiority, inadequacy, and low self-worth. This feeling shackles many Christians, in spite of wonderful spiritual experiences and knowledge of God's Word. Although they understand their position as sons and daughters of God, they are tied up in knots, bound by a terrible feeling of inferiority, and chained to a deep sense of worthlessness.[9]*

There's a great story about a chronically depressed man who went for help to the psychologist Carl Jung. Jung told the man to cut his fourteen-hour workdays back to eight, then go directly home and spend his evenings alone and quiet. So the man spent every evening behind closed doors, reading the works of Thomas Mann and Herman Hesse and playing Mozart and Chopin on his piano.

After a few weeks the depressed man returned to Jung, described what he'd been doing, and complained at his lack of improvement. Jung responded, "But you didn't understand. I didn't want you to be with Hesse or Mann or Chopin or Mozart. I wanted you to be completely alone."

The man looked horrified: "I can't think of any worse company."

Jung replied, "Yet this is the self you inflict on other people fourteen hours a day."[10]

That kind of self-hatred hangs like a cloud between Christians and the Father of Lights. We are horrified at the thought of a silent retreat. We are so immobilized by self-loathing that we neutralize God's Spirit in us, choking off the nourishment meant to make us grow and blossom and bear fruit.

We are so immobilized by self-loathing that we neutralize God's Spirit in us.

We hear the voices of overpowering adults, moralizing church folk, cruel peers, disloyal friends. Even the one who stares back from the mirror reflects nothing but judgment and lame excuses:

"You'll never amount to anything."

"You'll never grow up."

"You're just like your father."

"How can you live like that?"

"Don't quit your day job."

No wonder so many of us just want to be sedated. Alcohol and other depressants will do the trick. As will overachieving and every form of people pleasing. So will comfort food and quick fixes that make the blood sugar spike, and stimulants that make the heart race and muck around with sight, sound, taste, touch, and hearing. So will hooking up. And so will cutting and all manner of self-abuse if the pain gets bad enough.

Henri Nouwen wrote,

> *I have come to realize that the greatest trap in our life is not success, popularity, or power, but self-rejection. Success, popularity, and power can indeed present a great temptation, but their seductive quality often comes from the way they are part of the much larger temptation to self-rejection. When we have come to believe in the voices that call us worthless and unlovable, then success, popularity, and power are easily perceived as attractive solutions. The real trap, however, is self-rejection. . . . Self-rejection is the greatest enemy of the spiritual life because it contradicts the sacred voice that calls us the "Beloved." Being the Beloved constitutes the core truth of our existence.*[11]

We learn to be gentle with ourselves by experiencing the intimate, heart-to-heart compassion of Jesus. When he is at home in our hearts he brings light and warmth and, bit by bit, renovation, until the dark fortress becomes a palace.

All that begins when we abandon self-hatred and start believing Jesus when he claims to know us better than we know ourselves. And really, it doesn't begin a minute sooner.

SOLITUDE

In the summer of 1992 I lived twenty days in a cabin in the Colorado Rockies. My retreat combined counseling therapy, personal silence, and except for my counselor, complete solitude. It was a giant step on my inward journey. Early each morning I met with a psychologist who helped recover repressed memories and feelings from my childhood. The remainder of each day I was alone in the cabin: no television, no music, no reading.

As the days passed, I realized I had not been able to really *feel* anything since I was eight years old, when a traumatic experience shut down my memory for the next nine years and my feelings for the next five decades.

When I was eight, The Poser—my fake self—was born as a defense against pain. The Poser within whispered, "Brennan, don't ever be your real self anymore because nobody likes you as you are. Invent a new self that everybody will admire but nobody will truly know." I took his advice. I became a good boy—polite, well-mannered, inconspicuous, and compliant. I studied hard, scored excellent grades, won a college scholarship, and was stalked every waking minute by the terror of abandonment and the sense that no one was there for me.

It worked, for the most part. I learned that perfect performance brought the recognition and approval I craved. But the appearance of perfection is difficult to maintain, and I was still afraid. So I slipped into an orbit of unfeeling to keep fear and shame at a safe distance.

The Poser obliged by taking care of all my public appearances with breezy charm. He kept me going when I might have given up. He carried me through two decades as a priest, skillfully separating my heart from my head. A scene in the movie *Postcards from the Edge* says it all. A film star is reminded by her director what a wonderful life she's had and how any woman would envy her accomplishments. "Yes, I know," the actor says, "but you know what? I can't feel any of my life. I've never been able to feel my life and all those good things."[12] I understand. For eighteen years I proclaimed the good news of God's passionate, unconditional love—utterly convinced in my head without ever feeling God's love in my heart. My therapist observed, "All these years there has been a steel trapdoor covering your emotions and denying you access to them."

On the tenth day of my mountain retreat I found myself crying, then sobbing. As my grief spilled out, a remarkable thing happened: In the distance I heard music and dancing. I was the prodigal son limping home—not to be a spectator but a participant in my Abba's love. The Poser faded, and I got in touch with my true self as the returned child of God. My craving for praise and affirmation began to shrink.

As Mary Michael O'Shaughnessy likes to say, "Often breakdowns lead to breakthroughs." I came to see that my emotional detachment grew because I refused to mourn the loss of a soft word and a tender embrace in childhood. "You're blessed when you feel you've lost what is most dear to you. Only then can you be embraced by the One most dear to you."[13]

It used to be that I never felt safe with myself unless I was performing flawlessly. My desire to be perfect was greater than my desire for God. Bullied by an all-or-nothing standard of my own making, I interpreted weakness as mediocrity and inconsistency as a loss of nerve. I thought compassion and self-acceptance were self-indulgent. Eventually I just wore myself out. My sense of personal failure and inadequacy stripped my self-esteem bare, triggering episodes of mild depression and wild anxiety.

My desire to be perfect was greater than my desire for God.

Without intending it, I projected onto God my feelings about myself. I felt safe with him only when I saw myself as noble, generous, and loving, free of scars, fears, and tears—*perfect!*

Over the years it had become harder and harder to show my true face. But on that bright morning in a cabin deep in the Rockies, I came out of hiding. Jesus removed my cloak of perfectionism and, feeling forgiven, free, and safe, I ran home to Abba. Finally I knew that I *knew* Someone was there for me. Gripped to the depth of my heart, tears rolling down my cheeks, I embraced and finally *felt* all the words I've written and spoken about God's stubborn, relentless Love. That morning I understood that words are just vapor compared to the Reality. I leapt from teaching God's love to really believing I am Abba's delight.

What does it mean to feel safe? That same afternoon I wrote in my journal:

> *To feel safe is to stop living in my head and sink down into my heart and feel liked and accepted . . . not having to hide anymore and distract myself with books, television, movies, ice cream, shallow conversation . . . staying in the present moment and not escaping into the past or projecting into the future, alert and attentive to the now . . . feeling relaxed and not nervous or jittery . . . no need to impress or dazzle others or draw attention to myself. . . . Unselfconscious, a new way of being with myself, a new way of being in the world . . . calm, unafraid, no anxiety about what's going to happen next . . . loved and valued . . . just being together as an end in itself.*

THE CATCH

Here's the catch, for me at least. Writing about that experience now, I risk inventing a new Poser with an even subtler disguise. "Hey," he whispers, "look how humble you've become. Isn't that great? Look how God has made you an example of his grace. You have so much to offer now that you've truly arrived. Don't mess that up; don't let anyone get close enough to suspect you're not totally humble every minute of every day." Reflecting on the kind of encounter with God I had in my mountain retreat, I thought of Teresa of Avila's sobering words: "Such experiences are given to the weaker brothers and sisters to fortify their flagging faith." I can twist giving credit to "the grace of God" into a self-promoting cliché so fast it makes my head spin. Weaker brother? That seems fair enough to me.

Thomas Merton told a fellow monk, "If I make anything out of the fact that I am Thomas Merton, I am dead. And if you make anything out of the fact that you are in charge of the pig barn, you are dead." Merton's solution? "Quit keeping score altogether and surrender yourself with all your sinfulness to God who sees neither the score nor the scorekeeper but only his child redeemed by Christ."[14]

Quit keeping score. That part is difficult as long as we keep hoping that, in spite of everything, we'll somehow turn out to be winners after all (and our enemies, of course, will turn out to be losers).

Sorry, that's not how it works.

This is how it works: All things work together for those who love God, "even," Augustine of Hippo added, "our sins." And not just our sins. The God who forgives and forgets our wrongdoing also turns our weakness to strength:

*Now I take limitations in stride, and with good cheer, these lim-
itations that cut me down to size—abuse, accidents, opposi-
tion, bad breaks. I just let Christ take over! And so the weaker
I get, the stronger I become.*[15]

Thornton Wilder's play *The Angel That Troubled the Waters* is set at the
pool of Bethesda, the site of an encounter between Jesus and a crippled
man in John 5:1-4. People come to this fountain because they believe
an angel sometimes stirs the water and the first person in the pool after
the angel's touch will be healed. In Wilder's play, a doctor comes, longing to be healed of his depression. When the angel appears he keeps
the doctor from stepping into the water. The physician begs the angel
for help but the angel says this moment is not for him:

*Without your wounds where would your power be? It is your
melancholy that makes your low voice tremble into the hearts of
men and women. The very angels themselves cannot persuade
the wretched and blundering children on earth as can one
human being broken on the wheels of living. In Love's service,
only wounded soldiers can serve. Physician, draw back.*

Without your wounds where would your power be?

Later, the man who stepped into the water while the physician was
restrained approaches to say:

*Please come with me. It is only an hour to my home. My son
is lost in dark thoughts. I do not understand him and only you
have ever lifted his mood. Only an hour. . . . There is also my*

daughter: since her child died, she sits in the shadow. She will
not listen to us but she will listen to you.[16]

"In Love's service, only wounded soldiers can serve." Pretending we have no wounds is a self-absorbed lie. And not just self-absorbed but self-defeating. When fear and shame drive me to conceal my wounds, it's not just others I keep in the dark. So why is it so easy to hang onto my bad feelings and pain when what I should do is let go?

Dietrich Bonhoeffer said guilt is an idol, and he was right because some of us can't get enough of our guilt, and "Whatever you can't get enough of, that's your god."[17]

But guilt? Why would a person worship at the altar of guilt? Because it is *her* guilt and no one can take it from her? Because it gives shape to her life? Because, in the end, it's about *her*? "Whatever you can't get enough of, that's your god."

As long as we pretend we're too good to need forgiveness, or too bad to receive it, we live in lonely parallel to other people's lives without ever truly meeting them. When we dare to live as if the true God's forgiveness is good enough for us, then and only then do our lives merge with all the wounded healers who draw ever closer to Jesus.

SPIN DOCTOR

Alcoholics Anonymous is a community of wounded healers. Psychiatrist James Knight wrote, "The effectiveness of AA's members in the care and treatment of their fellow alcoholics is one of the great success stories of our time, and graphically illustrates the power of wounds, when used creatively, to lighten the burden of pain and suffering."[18]

Why Alcoholics Anonymous more than the Christian communities? Maybe just this: People who enter the community of Alcoholics Anonymous enter because their lives have become unmanageable. Most of the rest of us will never admit our lives are unmanageable, and The Poser will back us up on that. The Poser is all about risk management and, when necessary, damage control. The Poser is a handler, a spin doctor, a fixer, a cleanup artist — he'll do whatever it takes to maintain the appearance that we are not out of control, that our lives are not unmanageable, that we are not in need of a Rescuer.

But The Poser knows that's a lie. Huddling here in the dark, we know it too.

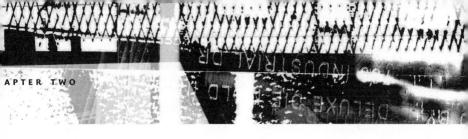

THE POSER

Leonard Zelig has no idea who he is.

Zelig is Woody Allen's creation, a mutating twentieth-century celebrity with a unique, lizardlike ability to change his appearance, voice, even his language, to fit any situation—whether he belongs there or not. Zelig crashes the party at a ticker-tape parade in 1930s New York; he shows up for a presidential photo-op, standing between Herbert Hoover and Calvin Coolidge; he clowns with prizefighter Jack Dempsey; he talks theater with playwright Eugene O'Neill; he's on the speakers' platform in Germany with uber-villain Adolf Hitler.[1]

Zelig is master of a thousand disguises. He blends into a cluster of Chinese nationals. Encountering Jewish rabbis, he spontaneously sprouts a beard and side curls. Thrown in with psychiatrists, he opens his mouth and out comes a stream of psychobabble. He's a priest when he tours the Vatican, a black man when he visits a jazz club, then Mohawk at a gathering of tribal chiefs.

Leonard Zelig has no personality, no ideas, no opinions of his own. He's a shape-shifter who blends in everywhere . . . and nowhere. He wants to fit in, to be accepted, to be liked, to feel safe. But day after day he settles for *seeming* to belong. Leonard Zelig becomes world famous in Woody Allen's film, but for what? A unique talent or a tragic flaw? Zelig is famous for being nobody.

It would be easy to giggle at Woody Allen's wit and move on—if I weren't so much like Leonard Zelig myself. I'm a Poser too. I'm not a shape-shifter, but I have a mask for every occasion. At my worst, I'm not much more than a mirror held up so people see a faint reflection of themselves when they look at me. I hope they like what they see. That is, of course, why I do it: to be liked.

The Poser in me trembles at the thought of disappointing people. Fear makes him incapable of direct speech. He hedges, waffles, procrastinates. The Poser is scared silent by the threat of rejection.

The Poser in me trembles at the thought of disappointing people.

My fake self protects me like Leonard Zelig's fake self protected him, but "in a way that is programmed to keep us fearful of being abandoned, losing support, not being able to cope on our own," in James Masterson's words, "not being able to be alone."[2] That's the story of my life.

For years I prided myself on punctuality. But in the solitude of my Colorado retreat, I realized I want to be on time mainly because I fear human disapproval. The right thing done for the wrong reason—to quiet the scolding voices from my childhood.

Posers are frantic for approval. We have an almost suffocating need to please, which makes it difficult to say *no*, even when *no* is the right answer. Posers are habitually overcommitted to people, projects, and causes, and we're habitually unhappy about that because our involvement has less to do with personal commitment than with the fear of not living up to expectations. The sick thing is we usually get what we wanted because who doesn't like a person who always says *yes?* That's a question The Poser hopes will never get a straight answer.

For most of us The Poser first shows up in childhood when we are not loved well or feel rejected or abandoned. John Bradshaw defines codependency as a condition "characterized by a loss of identity. To be codependent," he says, "is to be out of touch with one's feelings, needs, and desires."[3] That makes The Poser a classic codependent.

Posers bury or disguise our true feelings to get what we want. Which makes emotional honesty impossible. Posers are driven by a compulsive desire to appear perfect. We hope everyone will admire us and no one will truly know us. The Poser's life is a roller-coaster ride of giddy highs and heart-dropping lows.

The fake self counts on outside experiences to deliver inner meaning. Money, power, physical attraction, sexual conquest, achievement, recognition, status — that's all Posers want and the last thing we need because a little success encourages illusions of self-importance and promises continued good fortune.

The fake self counts on outside experiences to deliver inner meaning.

HUMAN BEING OR HUMAN DOING?

As far as he knows, The Poser is what he *does*.

For a long time I hid from my true self by performing in ministry. I constructed a fake identity through sermons, books, and storytelling. I convinced myself that if the majority of Christians thought well of me, there was nothing wrong, right? The more ministerial success I experienced, the more convincing The Poser became.

The Poser attaches importance where there is none and puts glitter on what's least substantial to distract us from what's real and true. He feeds us reasons for not doing the right thing and a million excuses when we do wrong. If we believe The Poser's lies, it's just a matter of time till we can no longer remember the truth about our own hollowness. As John put it: "If we claim that we're free of sin, we're only fooling ourselves. A claim like that is errant nonsense."[4]

Craving the approval I missed in childhood, my fake self wakes up every day starved for attention. When I give in to him, I pull a cardboard mask over my true face and enter a roomful of people with a trumpet blast: "Ta-da! Here I am!" That's so unlike my true self, hidden with Christ in God, who enters a room saying, "Oh, there *you* are!" The Poser is a lot like alcohol for the alcoholic—cunning, baffling, powerful, intoxicating, and treacherous.

In Susan Howatch's novel *Glittering Images*, a young theologian named Charles Ashworth undergoes a moral meltdown. Longing for the blessing of his own father, Ashworth goes to a monastery to meet with his spiritual director, an older man named Jon Darrow. Ashworth is frightened of being exposed as a corrupt clergyman and a spiritual failure. Cunningly, The Poser intervenes:

> *The thought of abject failure was appalling enough, but the thought of disappointing Darrow was intolerable. In panic I cast around for a solution which would protect me in my vulnerability, and when Darrow returned to my room that evening, the glittering image said to him: "I do wish you would tell me more about yourself, Father. There's so much I'd like to know." As soon as the words were spoken, I felt myself relaxing. This was an infallible technique for acquiring the good will of older men. I would ask them about their past, I would listen with the ardent interest of the model disciple and I would be rewarded by a gratifying display*

of paternal benevolence which would be blind to all the faults and
failings I was so desperately anxious to conceal. "Tell me about
your days in the Navy!" I urged Darrow with all the warmth
and charm I could muster, but although I waited with confidence
for the response which would anesthetize my fear of unfitness,
Darrow was silent. . . . Another silence fell as I painfully per-
ceived the machinations of my glittering image.[5]

PRETENSE

The Poser is preoccupied with appearance. If I binge on a pint of
Häagen-Dazs Peanut Butter Vanilla and the bathroom scale registers an
extra pound the next morning, The Poser freaks out. A sunny day
invites me out to play, but that extra pound is a deal breaker for the self-
absorbed Poser who wants me to hide indoors. I guess it's possible Jesus
smiles at these ridiculous vanities (checking myself out in a storefront
window while pretending to look at merchandise); maybe he winces.
What I know for certain is, vanity hijacks my attention from the God
who loves me and lives in me and vanity robs me—for how long? a
moment? a day? a whole summer?—of the joy of God's Holy Spirit.
Still, my fake self rationalizes this obsession with my appearance, whispering, "A fat, sloppy image disqualifies you for ministry." Cunning.

Vanity hijacks my attention from the God who loves me and lives in me.

I don't think I'm alone in this. The time, energy, cash, and discipline
necessary to acquire and maintain a finely tuned body image is so stag-
gering it's simply beyond many people; they just give up on it. Way
beyond valid health concerns, the obsessed leave no snack unplanned,
no nibble spontaneous, no calorie, carb, or fat gram uncharted. Weight

control is a near-religious expression with its own professional priesthood laying down the law, sacred books and devotionals for daily guidance, pilgrimages to holy health spas, and weighty theological discussions of the high-protein diet. And in the end, if we can afford it, a nip here, a tuck there, covers a multitude of sins, not the least of which is the sin of maturing from one age to the next. What is spiritual ecstasy compared to the exquisite pleasure of looking like a runway model? To paraphrase Cardinal Wolsey, "Would that I had served my God the way I have watched my waistline."

The Poser demands attention. In his craving for compliments, appearance drives every choice. He turns the Latin virtue *esse quam videri* (to be, rather than to seem to be) upside down so that "seeming to be" is all he asks. For The Poser, it's not whether you win or lose, it's how you look playing the game.

For The Poser, it's not whether you win or lose, it's how you look playing the game.

Midway through a book, I noticed the author had quoted something I wrote. I felt an instant flush of gratification and a rush of self-importance. When I turned to Jesus in prayer and got in touch with my true self, I saw yet again, The Poser lurks everywhere!

Thomas Merton admitted:

> *My false and private self is the one who wants to exist outside the reach of God's will and God's love—outside of reality and outside of life. And such a self cannot help but be an illusion. We are not very good at recognizing illusions, least of all the ones we cherish about ourselves—the ones we were born with*

*and which feed the roots of sin. For most people in the world,
there is no greater subjective reality than this false self of theirs,
which cannot exist. A life devoted to the cult of this shadow is
what is called a life of sin.*[6]

Merton's idea of sin focuses not so much on individual acts as the underlying choice to live a life of pretense. "There can only be two basic loves," wrote Augustine, "the love of God unto the forgetfulness of self, or the love of self unto the forgetfulness and denial of God." The fundamental choice happens in the *core* of our being, then plays itself out in the specific choices of daily living—either for the fake self ruled by self-centered desires or for the true self hidden with Christ in God.

PUTTIN' ON THE RITZ

Posers draw their identities not only from achievements but from parasitic relationships. Posers pursue relationships with those who will make them look good. To posers, relationships *are* achievements.

Posers pursue relationships with those who will make them look good.

One lonely night in the Colorado Rockies, I heard this message: "Brennan, you bring your full presence and attention to certain members of the community but offer very little to others. Those who have stature, wealth, and charisma, those you find interesting or charming or pretty or famous command your undivided attention. But people you consider plain or frumpy, those of low rank, performing humble tasks, the unsung and uncelebrated, you do not treat with the same regard. This is not a minor matter to me, Brennan. The way you are with others every day, regardless of their status, is the true test of faith."

Later in the evening as I dozed off, conflicting images danced across the screen of my mind: Carlton Hayes, a magnificently chiseled athlete in his early twenties, six-foot-three, 185 pounds, bounces on a trampoline flashing his irresistible smile. A crowd gathers. Now he is skipping rope — a dazzling display of agility and grace. The onlookers cheer. "Praise God!" the athlete shouts.

Jump cut to Moe, part of Carlton's entourage, as he approaches with an energy drink. Moe is in his fifties, just five-foot-four and thick around the middle. He wears a rumpled suit with a dingy T-shirt visible where his shirt gaps. Thin slivers of matted hair extend from Moe's temples over his ears and disappear in a clump of gray-black at the back of his head. He needs a shave, his face is puffy, he has a glass eye. Spectators glance at Moe and their eyes dart away.

"Loser," one man says.

"Brown-nose," says another.

Moe is neither. Moe's heart is buried with Christ in the Father's love. He moves unselfconsciously through the crowd to extend the sports bottle to the hero. He is as comfortable with his servant role as a hand in a glove (that is how Jesus first revealed himself to Moe and transformed his life). Moe feels safe with himself because he is safe with God.

That night, Carlton Hayes will deliver the main address to an adoring crowd gathered from all fifty states for the Fellowship of Christian Athletes national banquet. He will be honored with a Waterford crystal cup as the first eight-time Olympic gold medalist.

Five thousand people assemble at the Ritz-Carlton Hotel. Glitterati from the worlds of politics, sports, and entertainment are scattered throughout the room. As Hayes steps to the podium, the crowd is just finishing a sumptuous meal. His address overflows with references to the power of Christ and shameless gratitude to God. Their hearts touched, men and women weep openly and then respond with a standing ovation.

But look behind his glossy delivery and Carlton's vacant stare reveals that his words do not inhabit his soul. Stardom has chipped away at his presence with Jesus. Real intimacy with God is just a memory. The Spirit's whispering has been drowned out by deafening applause.

Riding a wave of affection from the crowd, the Olympic hero moves easily from table to table. He kisses up to everyone—from the waiters to the movie stars. He can afford to: He's got them eating out of his hand.

Back at the Red Roof Inn, Moe sits down to a frozen dinner at the little round table in his room. He was not invited to the banquet at the Ritz-Carlton because, frankly, Moe doesn't fit in. Who would even consider inviting the greasy-haired, potbellied, glass-eyed hireling to pull up a chair with the likes of Bruce Willis, Arnold Schwarzenegger, and former President Bush?

Moe closes his eyes. The love of Jesus surges within him. His eyes fill with tears. "Thank you, Jesus," he whispers, as he peels the plastic top off his microwaved lasagna. He flips to Psalm 23 in his Bible:

> GOD, *my shepherd!*
>> *I don't need a thing.*
> *You have bedded me down in lush meadows,*
>> *you find me quiet pools to drink from.*

I am in the dream too. The Poser has acquired tuxes from who knows where so we can attend the banquet at the Ritz.

///

The next morning I awoke in the cabin at 4:00 A.M., showered, shaved, fixed a cup of coffee, and thumbed through the Bible. My eyes fell on a passage in 2 Corinthians:

> *Our firm decision is to work from this focused center: One man died for everyone. That puts everyone in the same boat. He included everyone in his death so that everyone could also be included in his life, a resurrection life, a far better life than people ever lived on their own.*
>
> *Because of this decision we don't evaluate people by what they have or how they look. We looked at the Messiah that way once and got it all wrong, as you know. We certainly don't look at him that way anymore.*[7]

Yikes! Even in my dreams. God help me, I lug this fake self around even in my dreams.

SCARED SILENT

I relate to Charles Ashworth, the character in the Howatch novel, when his spiritual director comments, "Charles, would I be reading too much into your remarks if I deduced that liking and approval are very important to you?"

"Well, of course they're important," Ashworth exclaims. "Aren't they important to everyone? Isn't that what life's all about? Success is people liking and approving of you. Failure is being rejected. Everyone knows that."[8]

The sad irony is that The Poser is incapable of true intimacy in any relationship. His self-love excludes others. Living so far out of touch with his own feelings, intuitions, and insights makes The Poser that much less sensitive to the moods, needs, and dreams of others. Give and take is out of the question. Whether he knows it or not, The Poser only gives to take. He's convinced he's only taking what he needs, what's rightly his to take.

Merton said a life devoted to the shadow is a life of sin. If that's true, I have sinned in my cowardly refusal—out of fear of rejection—to think, feel, act, respond, and live from my authentic self. Of course, The Poser "argues relentlessly that the root of the problem is minor and should be ignored, that 'mature' men and women would not get so upset over something so trivial, that one's equilibrium should be maintained even if it means placing unreasonable limits on personal hopes and dreams and accepting life in a diminished form."[9]

I have sinned in my cowardly refusal—out of fear of rejection—to think, feel, act, respond, and live from my authentic self.

If you told The Poser, "No, you're just a coward," he would be shocked, hurt, and angry. But you would be right. As a child I could cop a plea, claiming I was powerless and afraid. Now in the autumn of my life, strengthened by so much love and affection and endless affirmation, I have to admit, painfully, that I still operate out of fear. I have been speechless in the face of conspicuous injustice. I've let The Poser do the talking while the real me took a passive role in relationships, smothered my own creativity, denied my true feelings, allowed myself to be intimidated by others, and then excused my behavior by saying it's okay because the Lord wants me to be an instrument of peace. . . . Oh, really? Is that the story you're going with?

YOUR OWN MISTAKE

It gets worse. We even withhold our true selves from God—and then wonder why we're not feeling the love. It's a crazy strategy that can only hurt us because we were made for intimacy with God. Whatever we do to interrupt that just makes us feel less human, less like ourselves. We are made for God, and nothing less will satisfy us.

Jeffrey Imbach wrote, "Prayer is essentially the expression of our heart longing for love. It is not so much the listing of our requests but the breathing of our own deepest request, to be united with God as fully as possible."[10]

So, have you ever felt baffled by your internal resistance to praying? By your dread of silence, solitude, and being alone with God? By your foot-dragging and falling asleep and the endless petty distractions that hijack your prayers?

Have you ever felt baffled by your internal resistance to praying?

The Poser strikes again! He is the lazy, corner-cutting part of us. He resists the effort and discipline that intimacy with God requires. He makes up lame excuses like, "Just let it flow . . . If you love God, that's all that matters . . . You're busy . . . What ever happened to spontaneity?" What a weasel.

The Poser dreads solitude because somehow he knows, "that if he would become silent within and without he would discover himself to be nothing. He would be left with nothing but his own nothingness, and to the false self which claims to be everything, such a discovery would be his undoing."[11]

Obviously, The Poser is antsy when you try to pray. He has an appetite for adventure and mood-altering excitement. He gets depressed when there's no spotlight. The fake self is frustrated because he never hears God's voice, which of course he cannot, since God sees no one there. A life of praying means death to every identity that does not come from God. The fake self runs from solitude because it reminds him of this unbearable truth: "There is no substance under the things with which you are clothed. You are hollow and your structure of pleasure and ambitions has no foundation. . . . And when they are gone there will be nothing left of you but your own nakedness and emptiness and hollowness, to tell you that you are your own mistake."[12] So. How do you like them apples?

ONE THING LEADS TO ANOTHER

Is all this self-examination really necessary?

Not exactly. This is how the writer Annie Dillard sees it:

> God does not demand that we give up our personal dignity, that we throw in our lot with random people, that we lose ourselves and turn from all that is not him. . . . It is a life with God which demands these things.
>
> Experience has taught the race that if knowledge of God is the end, then these habits of life are not the means but the condition in which the means operates. . . . You do not have to do these things—unless you want to know God. They work on you, not on him.[13]

If knowing God and becoming your true self were of no interest to you there would be nothing to worry about. But the fact that you've read this far suggests you do care. If that's true, then much sooner than later, it's time to call The Poser out of hiding, accept him, embrace him, and bring him to Jesus.

It's time to call The Poser out of hiding, accept him, embrace him, and bring him to Jesus.

"Excuse me, did you just say accept and embrace The Poser?"

I did say that, yes—and bring him to Jesus. Because whatever is denied can't be healed. The Poser is part of us. Admitting how often we escape to our own little kingdoms, how we trivialize our relationship with God, how ambition drives us—admitting all this is a blow against the empire. But one blow won't do the trick for most of us. We have to haul The Poser into the light of Christ's presence day after day until the false king is deposed and the kingdoms of this world become the kingdom of our Lord and of his Christ.

We have to acknowledge our selfishness and stupidity and gradually accept that we're as poor and broken as the next guy. And that it's okay because if we weren't then we would be God.

I can't speak for you, but all the evidence points to the fact that there is a God and that it's definitely not me. Interestingly enough, this is where things lighten up a bit. If I'm not God, then the expectation that I should be perfect is off the table. If I'm an ordinary human being—not much better or worse or really much different from my neighbor—there's nothing wrong with learning to be a little gentle toward myself and then a little gentle toward that neighbor. That's the order in which it occurs. The art of gentleness toward ourselves leads to gentleness with others. What's more, becoming gentle with ourselves generates the compassion necessary for real praying. The writer of the book of Hebrews says Jesus is sympathetic when he represents our needs to his Abba because Jesus understands our weakness. Once we admit who we truly are and how we truly need Jesus, we become sympathetic too, and that makes us much better pray-ers.

DEAR POSER

Accepting the reality of my brokenness means accepting my authentic self. Judas and Peter both betrayed Jesus. Judas could not face his shadow; Peter could. Peter's life changed; Judas ended his life. Neither outcome was a knee-jerk reaction to the circumstances. Each man decided he couldn't go on living that way. Their choices reflect the difference between the sorrow that leads a person to turn around and go the right way and the sorrow that leads to self-destruction. But not sudden self-destruction. "Suicide does not happen on a sudden impulse. It is an act that has been rehearsed during years of unconscious punitive behavior patterns."[14] In a way, suicide is meant to kill The Poser. Hatred of The Poser is actually self-hatred and, one way or another, self-hatred results in some kind of self-destructive behavior. And that's no good.

Carl Jung wrote:

> *The acceptance of oneself is the essence of the whole moral problem and the epitome of a whole outlook on life. That I feed the hungry, that I forgive an insult, that I love my enemy in the name of Christ—all these are undoubtedly great virtues. What I do unto the least of my brethren, that I do unto Christ. But what if I should discover that the least amongst them all, the poorest of all the beggars, the most impudent of all the offenders, the very enemy himself—that these are within me, and that I myself stand in need of the alms of my*

own kindness—that I myself am the enemy who must be loved—what then?[15]

When we accept the truth about ourselves and surrender it to Jesus Christ, we find peace—maybe not the constant emotional experience of peace, but genuine peace still, even when we don't understand it. Our true king says: *Silence the old voices in your head that bind you up and lock you down in self-centeredness. Listen to the new sound of salvation for people who know they're poor. Let go of your fear of Abba. Let go of your self-loathing. Learn to see things as they are. I love you, and that's enough. I am the son of compassion, and that's enough. You belong to Me, and that's enough.*

On the twentieth and last day of my stay in the Colorado Rockies, I wrote this letter:

Good morning, Poser.

You're probably surprised by the cordial greeting. I've hammered you from day one of this retreat, so you probably expected, "Hello, you little jerk." But that's not what I feel. I admit I've been unreasonable, ungrateful, and unbalanced about you. (Of course, you are aware, my little puff of smoke, that when I address you, I am talking to myself. You're a real part of me.) I come to you today not with a whip in my hand but with an olive branch. When I was young and first knew that no one was there for me, you intervened and showed me where to hide. It was The Great Depression of the thirties and my parents did the best they could with what they had—I know that—it just wasn't as much as I needed. At that time, you were invaluable. Without your intervention I would have

been overwhelmed by dread and paralyzed by fear. You protected me. Thank you.

But you also taught me how to hide my real self and
started a lifelong pattern of concealment and withdrawal. Your
resourcefulness enabled me to survive. But you lied to me.
"Brennan," you whispered, "if you insist on this folly of being
yourself, you'll lose the few friends you have. Stuff your feelings, shut down your memories, withhold your opinions, and
develop social graces so you'll fit in wherever you are."

You needed someone to put a saddle on you and harness
you. I didn't have what it took to tame you, so you grew stronger.
Your appetite for attention and affirmation was insatiable. I never
confronted you with the lie because I was deceived myself.

But now, in Christ's presence, you have already begun to
shrink. Wanna know something, little guy? You're much more
attractive that way. From now on I'm going to call you "Pee-
Wee." Naturally, you're not going to roll over and die. I know
you'll get agitated at times and start to act out, but the more
time you spend in the presence of Jesus, the less praise you'll need
from others because you will have discovered for yourself that
he is Enough. And in the Presence, you will delight in the discovery of what it means to live by grace and not by posing. So,
Pee-Wee, I remain,

Your friend,
Brennan

WHO'S YOUR DADDY?

It was a double-whammy. William Least Heat Moon found out he'd lost his job as a college professor because of declining enrollment. And he found out his wife had moved in with another man—sure, they were separated, but still. . . .

Instead of waiting around for more bad news, Moon set out to explore the back roads of North America—the "blue highways" on the map. One morning in the cafeteria at Mississippi College in Clinton,

> *a crewcut student wearing mesh step-in casuals sat down to a tall stack of pancakes. He was a methodical fellow. After a prayer running almost a minute, he pulled from his briefcase a Bible reading stand, clips to hold the book open, a green felt-tip, a pink, a yellow, next came a squeeze bottle of liquid margarine, a bottle of Log Cabin syrup wrapped in plastic, a linen napkin, and one of those little lemony wet-wipes. The whole business looked like the old circus where twelve men get out of a car the size of a trash can. . . . I thought he was going to pull out a Water-Pik and the Ark of the Covenant next.* [1]

What William Least Heat Moon saw that morning may have been a glimpse of that young man's true self—unselfconscious, unpretentious, immersed in life, absorbed in the present moment, breathing in God as naturally as a fish extracts oxygen from the water where it lives and moves. He witnessed that student just being himself—

slightly offbeat maybe, but like it or lump it, he wasn't trying to impress anyone.

Authentic spirituality is unselfconscious like that. It's not just a compartment to be visited on appropriate occasions: *Oh, I think I'll be spiritual now. I'm at church.* Or, *Oh I feel so spiritual when I watch a beautiful sunset.* Spirituality is a way of moving through the world immersed in the consciousness of God's presence in us and around and through us. The Poser can't enjoy true spirituality because he is absorbed by what *appears* to be rather than what is, because he's lost in himself rather than God. The Poser is stuck on what spirituality *looks* like.

As years in the monastery passed, Thomas Merton began to see that the highest spiritual development was to be *ordinary*, "to become fully a man, in the way few human beings succeed in becoming so simply and naturally themselves."[2]

DEAL WITH IT

John Eagan was an ordinary man—a high school teacher nobody outside Milwaukee ever heard of. Eagan spent thirty years developing kids. He never wrote a book, never appeared on television, never converted large numbers of people to faith, never gathered a reputation for holiness. John ate, slept, drank, biked cross-country, roamed the woods, taught classes—and prayed like crazy. And John kept a journal that tells the day-by-day story of an ordinary man whose soul was seduced and ravished by Jesus Christ.[3] John Eagan's journal demonstrates that it's not outside pressures, but we ourselves, that keep us from becoming all we're meant to be.

"We have met the enemy," Walt Kelly made Pogo, his comic-strip character, say—"We have met the enemy, and he is us." We judge ourselves unworthy to know and love and serve God, and that judgment becomes a self-fulfilling prophecy. We say we're too small to be used by God (though we also say God can make something from nothing). We say we're not smart enough, too weak, too inexperienced, too young. And somehow it seems what we say comes true, and we are not surprised when the God of miracles appears to do very little in and through us.

John Eagan was a flawed man, with conspicuous weaknesses and deep character defects, who learned that brokenness is in fact the human condition, that we must forgive ourselves for being unlovable, inconsistent, incompetent, irritable, and potbellied. And he learned that his own brokenness and wrongdoing could not keep him from God because all those things are reclaimed by the life and death and resurrection of Christ.

John turned away from The Poser, took his fake self to the Cross of Jesus, and dared to live as a truly forgiven man. John found out the term "Good Christian" is an oxymoron, like "jumbo shrimp" or "short sermon." In John Eagan's journal we hear echoes of Thomas Merton: "God is asking me, the unworthy, to forget my unworthiness and that of my brothers. . . . And to laugh, after all, at the preposterous ideas of 'worthiness'"[4]

Pursuing God through his life, Eagan prayed and meditated with intense discipline. On one of his annual eight-day, silent retreats, John was hammered by the revelation of his true self. On the morning of the sixth day, he was visiting with his spiritual director:

> *That day Bob says with great clarity, striking the table with his fist: ". . . John, this is your call, the way God is calling you. Pray for a deepening of this love, yes, savor the present*

moment where God is. Indulge the contemplative in you, sur-
render to it; let it be, search for God. . . . "

Then he states something that I will ponder for years; he
says it very deliberately. I ask him to repeat it so that I can
write it down. ". . . Define yourself radically as one beloved by
God. God's love for you and his choice of you constitute your
worth. Accept that, and let it become the most important thing
in your life."

We discuss it. The basis of my personal worth is not my
possessions, my talents, not esteem of others, reputation . . . not
kudos of appreciation from parents and kids, not applause, and
everyone telling you how important you are to the place. . . . I
stand anchored now in God before whom I stand naked, this
God who tells me "You are my son, my beloved one."[5]

This is the Big Idea: *Define yourself radically as one totally loved by God.*
Right now. As-Is. Not to be left like this, certainly, but just as certainly
never to be loved, valued, cherished any more or less than you are in
this very moment because God's love does not depend on you. So
please, please, please stop running away when you mess up, and run
into the arms of the one who totally loves you as you are right now.

This is the Big Idea: Define yourself radically as one totally loved by God.

Your ordinary self is exactly where God wants to work extraordinary miracles. The inconspicuous nobody who shivers when it's cold
and sweats when it's hot, who wakes up so many days feeling not-at-all-
ready to face the world, who can barely get dressed and show up on
time and at the right place, who has to read the paragraph three times
to understand it, who feels lonely and hopeless, isolated, crowded,

horny, left out, and taken in all at once — YOU are the one God loves! Deal with it.

THAT IS *SO* JUNIOR HIGH

The Poser searches for identity in praise for extraordinary effort: *If I do good, I am good*. If that fails, he settles for looking good: *It's not whether you win or lose, it's how you look playing the game*. Look amazing, feel amazing.

The true self finds identity in being totally loved by God in the ordinariness of life. The true self is grateful for spiritual highs without craving them and, likely as not, without making too much of them when they come. The true self knows we encounter God most often in the day-to-dayness of life.

Writing to an intellectual friend, Henri Nouwen said, "All I want to say to you is, 'You are the Beloved,' and all I hope is that you can hear these words as spoken to you with all the tenderness and force that love can hold. My only desire is to make these words reverberate in every corner of your being — 'You are the Beloved.'"[6] Once we drop anchor in that reality, our true self doesn't need a trumpet to announce our arrival or fireworks to hold people's attention. People who know they are totally loved seem to honor God just by showing up every day as nothing more than, or less than, or other than themselves.

This is not just a nice idea; this is our identity, you and me. Otherwise, we spend a lot of time wondering.

All George Foreman's children are called George. Does that strike you as odd? Well, odd or not, each child's name includes the name George, and that, of course, begs for an explanation. Before he was a one-man low-fat grilling powerhouse, George Foreman was heavyweight boxing champion of the world. And before that, a child who didn't know who his father was. And *that's* why all his kids are named George. It's not repeated blows to the head, and it's not a runaway ego. George Foreman says he always wants his children to know who their daddy is.

That's why your name, and mine, is *Abba's Child*.

If I seek an identity outside myself, then accumulating money, power, admiration, and fame attracts me, even if I know how upside down that is. Ironically, Christian churches often stroke The Poser by granting (and withholding) status based on what appears to be rather than what is. That's just crazy. But it explains why there's so much deadness in what's supposed to be the cradle of spiritual life. When we build social structures that reward some people for appearing to be better than others, how is that different from lunchtime at your typical junior high?

THIS IS ME ON A BAD DAY

"Who am I?" Thomas Merton asked, then answered his own question: "I am one loved by Christ."[7] How did he know that? He knew it the same way the theologian Karl Barth claimed to know it when a reporter asked him to say something profound about God. According to the story, Barth replied, "Jesus loves me/this I know/for the Bible tells me so."

It doesn't get much better than that. The intimate experience of total love starts in quiet conversation with the One who loves us. It begins with leaning in close enough to hear God's whisper, closing the door if necessary to shut out the noise, going outside if that's what it takes to escape the phone and computer and television and PlayStation and boom box—or maybe just going out for a walk together, Abba and Abba's Child. If someone watches you do that from a distance, it might look like you're reading a book, writing in a notebook, walking alone, maybe even talking to yourself. Sometimes it might seem that way to you as well. That's when it helps to think profound thoughts about God: *Jesus loves me/this I know/for the Bible tells me so.*

Our longing to know who we truly are will never be satisfied until we embrace solitude—not loneliness, that's a different thing—but genuine solitude where we discover that we are Totally Loved by God. No one can communicate that but the Abba who Totally Loves us. Oh, other people can say it, but God alone *communicates* how our true-self identity rests in his relentless tenderness. And he does that in private, after the music stops and the crowd goes home.

Our longing to know who we truly are will never be satisfied until we embrace solitude.

This may sound impossible if you live in an apartment, if your life is hyperscheduled from the moment you wake till you can't keep your eyes open anymore, if you are afraid to be quiet because your mind is, as Anne Lamott likes to say, a dangerous neighborhood where you wouldn't want to go alone.

Go there anyway. You can't change the world until you change your mind. Besides which, you won't really be alone. God will meet you there.

Mike Yaconelli traveled to Toronto for a five-day retreat because he was near the end of his rope. He went to L'Arche (The Ark), a community of profoundly handicapped people, where he hoped to find inspiration and perspective. He chose L'Arche mainly because it's where Henri Nouwen settled after he dropped out of the mainstream, and Mike hoped spending time with Nouwen would do the trick. But it wasn't Henri Nouwen Mike went to meet.

It only took being alone for a short period of time for me to dis-cover I wasn't alone. God had been trying to shout over the nois-iness of my life, and I couldn't hear him. But in the stillness and solitude, his whispers shouted from my soul, "Michael, I am here. I have been calling you, but you haven't been listening. Can you hear me, Michael? I love you. I have always loved you. And I have been waiting for you to hear me say that to you. But you have been so busy trying to prove to yourself you are loved that you have not heard me."

I heard him, and my slumbering soul was filled with the joy of the prodigal son. My soul was awakened by a loving Father who had been looking and waiting for me. Finally, I accepted my brokenness. . . . I had never come to terms with that. Let me explain. I knew I was broken. I knew I was a sin-ner. I knew I continually disappointed God, but I could never accept that part of me. It was a part of me that embarrassed me. I continually felt the need to apologize, to run from my weak-nesses, to deny who I was and concentrate on what I should be. . . .

At L'Arche, it became very clear to me that I had totally misunderstood the Christian faith. I came to see that it was in my brokenness, in my powerlessness, in my weakness that Jesus was made strong. It was in the acceptance of my lack of faith that God could give me faith. It was in the embracing of my brokenness that I could identify with others' brokenness. It was my role to identify with others' pain, not relieve it. Ministry was sharing, not dominating; understanding, not theologizing; caring, not fixing.

What does all this mean?

I don't know . . . and to be quite blunt, that is the wrong question. I only know that at certain times in all of our lives, we make an adjustment in the course of our lives. This was one of those times for me. If you were to look at a map of my life, you would not be aware of any noticeable difference other than a slight change in direction. I can only tell you that it feels very different now. There is an anticipation, an electricity about God's presence in my life that I have never experienced before. I can only tell you that for the first time in my life I can hear Jesus whisper to me every day, "Michael, I love you. You are beloved." And for some strange reason, that seems to be enough.[8]

I am struck by the directness, simplicity, and honesty of Yaconelli's words. It's clear The Poser didn't get a chance to edit.

A while back, deep under The Poser's spell, I wrote a book-jacket blurb for a fellow Poser's first published work. I defended his prose style saying, "His floridities are merely orotundity. Nevertheless, his unremitting gaseousness has an organic fluidity and turgescence difficult to duplicate and oddly purgative for the reader." What was I thinking!

I began a lecture on the eleventh step of the Alcoholics Anonymous program with a story about a man in crisis who notices and eats a strawberry. I was emphasizing his ability to live in the present moment. Then I launched into what I thought was a dazzling explanation of the eleventh step: "(We) Sought through prayer and meditation to improve our conscious contact with God as we understood him, praying only for knowledge of his will for us and the power to carry that out."

As the meeting ended, a woman approached the podium and said, "I loved your story about the strawberry." The strawberry? What about my dazzling explanation? But she was right. That humble strawberry carried far more meaning than my self-important rant.

Do you think it's a coincidence that the New Testament Gospels are written in plain, unpretentious language? The Gospels contain no trace of junk language, inside jargon, or doubletalk. (If the translation you've been reading isn't plainspoken, go find one that is—you'll know it when you see it.)

That style is so different from The Poser, who comes off like a cross between William Faulkner and the Marx Brothers. He talks about God in confusing, unnecessarily complicated, often goofy language to hide the truth that he doesn't really believe what God says at all. Because he's the master of disguise, The Poser imitates humble openness so you believe you're into his secret self when he hasn't actually disclosed anything about his true self. Once again, I didn't read this in a book; this is me on a bad day.

TRUE LOVE

"Alright, say I try this solitude thing. I close the door behind me, shut out the distractions. Then what do I do? What do I say?"

There's another journalist's story—this time with Mother Teresa— asking what she said when she prayed. "I don't say anything," she's reported to have answered.

"Okay," the journalist said, "well, what does God say to you?"

"God doesn't say anything," Teresa replied. "Praying is not about words." Maybe sensing doubt, she added, "If you don't understand that, I can't explain it to you." Of course she was right. How do you explain intimacy so another person understands? Intimacy can only be understood firsthand. And now you know today's homework. And tomorrow's.

When you've been splashing around in a pool, it takes time for the ripples to settle enough so you can see what's reflected there. Any attempt to speed the settling just creates new ripples. Learn to wait. Learn to be still, just a little at a time. You can't rush it. It takes however long it takes.

That means learning to ignore the voice that says you're wasting time. Theologian Edward Schillebeeckx says, "Silence with God has a value in itself and for its own sake, just because God is God. Failure to recognize the value of mere being with God, as the beloved, without doing anything, is to gouge the heart out of Christianity."[9]

If someone has promised you can have instant intimacy with God, without a serious investment of time and attention, I can only say you've been sincerely misled. It's the equivalent of a TV dating show where strangers find true love in six episodes. It doesn't happen that way. If their relationship survives to become true love, it happens after the show ends, when they take time to know each other and become truly (not just physically) intimate. True love grows more as it did in *The Princess Bride*, when it finally dawned on Buttercup that day after day and month after month, when Westley said, "As you wish," what he was really saying was, "I love you." And that's when Buttercup started to love him back.

SO WHO'S YOUR DADDY?

One more thing. If I'm distant from my true self, I am also distant from others. I've come to see that I connect best with others when I'm connected to the core of my true self. When I take my identity from God instead of other people, I find myself listening more attentively, loving more freely, acting with genuine compassion. And I'm more playful! I take myself less seriously when I feel my Abba's breath on my face. I find the truth in Anne Lamott's declaration that laughter is carbonated holiness.

I've come to see that I connect best with others when I'm connected to the core of my true self.

Intentionally "wasting" time with God enables me to speak and act from strength greater than my own, to forgive instead of nursing the bruise, to give without expecting to get back. All of which, you can see, makes me much more pleasant to be around.

From hound-dog disciples and sour-faced saints, spare us, O Lord! Frederick Buechner wrote,

> _Repent and believe in the gospel, Jesus says. Turn around and believe that the good news that we are loved is better than we ever dared hope, and that to believe in that good news, to live out of it and toward it, to be in love with that good news, is of all glad things in this world the gladdest thing of all. Amen, and come, Lord Jesus._ [10]

Frederick Buechner, John Eagan, Anne Lamott, Thomas Merton, Mike Yaconelli, the whole chorus of voices in this chapter, call us to stop running and start resting in God's promise that we are Totally Loved. You are _Abba's Child_. Every other identity is an illusion. "I am _Abba's Child._" This is your true self. _Abba's Child_. This is the final answer to the question, Who's your Daddy?

ABBA'S CHILD

The morning after. There's a note on my breakfast plate.

> *Dear Brennan,*
> *In all my eighty-three years, I have never had an experience like*
> *this. During your week of renewal here at Saint Cecelia's, you*
> *promised that if we attended each night, our lives would be*
> *changed. Mine has. Last week I was terrified at the prospect of*
> *dying; tonight I am homesick for the house of my Abba.*

I cried when I read it. Eighty-three years old. "Last week I was terrified at the prospect of dying; tonight I am homesick for the house of my Abba."

That idea—that God is our heavenly Abba, our Daddy—was brand new with Jesus. Jesus grew up in a religious culture where God's name was not spoken out loud or even spelled out completely. Not GOD, but G-D (only Hebrew, of course, not English). Does that seem odd to you? The notion that God loves us is hardly news to people in Western cultures. If people believe in God at all, they mostly believe in a God who loves us and tend to assume we're all children of God and brothers and sisters (no matter how badly we treat each other).

That's not what Jesus' neighbors thought. They thought about G-D as the Creator and Judge of humankind. They were all about the *transcendence* of G-D.

> *transcendent: 1a: exceeding usual limits : SURPASSING*
> *b: extending or lying beyond the limits of ordinary experience.*

The kids Jesus grew up with would have heard the line, "Father of orphans, champion of widows, is God in his holy house" from Psalm 68:5. They might have known Psalm 103:13: "As parents feel for their children, GOD feels for those who fear him." They may even have thought it was a nice metaphor. But Jesus didn't speak vaguely about "our Father," an idea that really occurs just once in the Old Testament (see Malachi 2:10). Jesus referred to God as "my Father" and he did it often (two dozen times in John's gospel).

And once, at least, he was overheard calling God his *Abba* — his *Papa* or *Daddy* (see Mark 14:35-36). That was — and is — a big deal. The neighbors never called their Creator *Abba*, because people who don't even spell out the name of G-D are unlikely to call him *Daddy*.[1]

The folks Jesus grew up around knew the prophetic psalms (Psalm 2 and Psalm 89) where G-D calls himself the Father of the future Hero King of Israel. So they took it badly when Jesus called G-D his personal Father because what he was saying was that he thought *he* was the Hero King they had been waiting for all those centuries.

Jesus' own family thought he was maybe just the least little bit whacko. Folks up in Capital City thought he was dangerous. When the case against Jesus went to trial in the middle of the night, the prosecutors said: "We have a law, and by that law he must die because he claimed to be the Son of God."[2] They seemed convinced Jesus meant something more than, "Oh, well, we're all children of God, you know? I mean, can't we all just get along?" Meanwhile, except for Judas, the people who had been hanging around with Jesus for years kept their fingers crossed that, unlikely as it seemed, when all was said and done God would turn out to be his Father after all.

Jesus' own family thought he was maybe just the least little bit whacko.

Those followers never forgot the intimacy between Jesus and his *Abba*. It was a central theme in the story they told, and it stuck with people wherever they told it. Paul, the highly mobile church-planter, told Christians in Rome:

> *This resurrection life you received from God is not a timid, gravetending life. It's adventurously expectant, greeting God with a childlike "What's next, Papa?" God's Spirit touches our spirits and confirms who we really are. We know who he is, and we know who we are: Father and children.*[3]

And John, the great pastor, wrote:

> *What marvelous love the Father has extended to us! Just look at it—we're called children of God! That's who we really are. But that's also why the world doesn't recognize us or take us seriously, because it has no idea who he is or what he's up to.*
>
> *But friends, that's exactly who we are: children of God.*[4]

WE GROW TENDER

I think this growing intimacy with God—this *Abba* experience—is the greatest gift I have received from Jesus. He said, "No one knows the Son the way the Father does, nor the Father the way the Son does. But

I'm not keeping it to myself; I'm ready to go over it line by line with anyone willing to listen."[5] Well, I'm listening. *Abba's Child* is who I am — that identity has become more valuable to me than any other.

When I try to manufacture a self-image from the praise of other people and The Poser whispers, "You've arrived; you're a player," I now know there's no truth in that self-concept. When I sink into depression and The Poser says, "Give it up. You're a fake. You're a hypocrite," I know there's no truth in that either. The psychologist Gerald May reminds us, "It is important to recognize these self-commentaries for the mind tricks they are. They have nothing to do with our real dignity. How we view ourselves at any given moment may have very little to do with who we really are."[6]

Beginning a silent retreat I journaled:

> *Wernersville, Pennsylvania, January 2 — Outside it's dark and below zero. That pretty well describes where I'm at inside. The opening night of an eight-day retreat and I'm filled with a sense of uneasiness, restlessness, even dread. Bone-weary and lonely. I can't connect two thoughts about God. Have abandoned any attempt at prayer: It seems too artificial. The few words spoken to God are forced and ring hollow in my empty soul. There is no joy being in his presence. An oppressive but vague feeling of guilt stirs within me. Somehow or other I have failed him. Maybe pride and vanity have blinded me; maybe insensitivity to pain has hardened my heart. Is my life a disappointment to you? Are you grieved by the shallowness of my soul? Whatever, I've lost you through my own fault and I am powerless to undo it. . . .*

Maybe not the world's best start for an annual retreat.

The physical exhaustion didn't last, but the spiritual dryness did. I groaned through two hours of lifeless prayer every morning, another two hours in the afternoon, then two more at night. I felt scatter-brained, disoriented, like I was rowing with one oar in the water. I read the Bible. Nothing there for me. I paced the floor. Monotony. I tried reading a Bible commentary. Zero.

On the afternoon of the fifth day, I went to the chapel at four o'clock and settled into a straight-backed chair to commence "the great stare"—meditation.

And for the next thirteen hours I remained wide awake, motionless, utterly alert. At ten minutes after five the next morning I left the chapel with one phrase ringing in my head and pounding in my heart: *Live in the wisdom of accepted tenderness.*

Tenderness comes alive when we know someone we care about is just knocked-out-crazy about us. Just knowing that person is in the room gives us a strong sense of safety and courage. The Poser's defense mechanisms—sarcasm, name-dropping, self-righteousness, being impressive—simply fall away. We become more open, real, vulnerable, and genuinely affectionate. We grow tender.

Tenderness comes alive when we know someone we care about is just knocked-out-crazy about us.

TO THE VERY LAST MOMENT

How would you respond if I asked you this question: "Do you honestly believe God likes you—not just loves you because God *has* to love you—but truly likes you?" If you get convinced from the top of your cap to the soles of your slip-ons that your Abba loves, cares, and yes!

LIKES you, you'll start experiencing a calm and tender compassion for yourself that changes—well, *everything*.

God's story suggests that *compassion* is the essence of his nature and *tenderness* is his heartbeat.

> *Through the heartfelt mercies of our God,*
> > *God's Sunrise will break in upon us,*
> *Shining on those in the darkness,*
> > *those sitting in the shadow of death,*
> *Then showing us the way, one foot at a time,*
> > *down the path of peace.*[7]

> *Can a mother forget the infant at her breast,*
> > *walk away from the baby she bore?*
> *But even if mothers forget,*
> > *I'd never forget you—never.*
> *Look, I've written your names on the backs of my hands.*[8]

Richard Foster wrote, "His heart is the most sensitive and tender of all. No act goes unnoticed, no matter how insignificant or small. A cup of cold water is enough to put tears in the eyes of God. Like the proud mother who is thrilled to receive a bouquet of wilted dandelions from her child, so God celebrates our feeble expressions of gratitude."[9] God is, perhaps, more tender than you know.

Jesus understands the tenderness of his Abba's heart. He is the first-born of Abba's children. Why did Jesus love all those career sinners and moral ragamuffins in the Gospels? Because his Abba loved them. He did nothing on his own, Jesus said, but only what his Abba told him.

Through eating and drinking, preaching, teaching, and healing, Jesus demonstrated his Father's extravagant love—love that makes the sun rise and the rain fall on the good, the bad, and the ugly.

In these acts of love Jesus created a scandal for devout first-century Jews:

> *The absolutely unpardonable thing was not his concern for the sick, the cripples, the lepers, the possessed . . . not even his partnership for the poor, humble people. The real trouble was that he got involved with moral failures, with obviously irreligious and immoral people; people morally and politically suspect, so many dubious, obscure, abandoned, hopeless types. . . . What kind of dangerous and naive love is this, which does not know its limits: the frontiers between fellow countrymen and foreigners, party members and non-members, between neighbors and distant people, between honorable and dishonorable callings, between moral and immoral, good and bad people?*[10]

The rising sun and the falling rain are gifts to those who love God and those who don't. And the compassion of Jesus embraces the worst among us and opens the way for people still living in sin. The Judge-and-Jury who lives in all of us shuns anyone whose sin we don't understand (if I understand a sin, it's a character flaw and a struggle; if I don't understand it, it's a perversion, right?). Jesus turns toward the perverse with gracious kindness, and he keeps paying attention throughout their lives for the sake of their conversions, "which is always possible to the very last moment."[11]

The compassion of Jesus embraces the worst among us and opens the way for people still living in sin.

COMPASSION

> *What marvelous love the Father has extended to us! Just look at it—we're called children of God! . . . And that's only the beginning. Who knows how we'll end up! What we know is that when Christ is openly revealed, we'll see him—and in seeing him, become like him. All of us who look forward to his Coming stay ready, with the glistening purity of Jesus' life as a model for our own.* [12]

The pastor John wrote that to say this: The highest, most demanding call in our lives is becoming like Jesus.

The highest, most demanding call in our lives is becoming like Jesus.

Happily we're not in it alone. It's not just copying what Jesus would do. (The Poser would like that, wouldn't he?) It's the very life of Jesus flowing in us and through us and out of us because God's Spirit has taken up residence in the heart of us. We can be, in the best possible way, under the influence of the Holy Spirit, we can be intoxicated by the Spirit of Christ every bit as much as a person can get drunk on wine coolers (but with completely different results).

That said, The Poser—who resists giving up control even to God—gets nervous when we talk like this. Saint Irenaeus said God took on our humanness so that we might become like God. Thanks in part to The Poser, this has meant different things to different people across the centuries. Where people think of God primarily as all-knowing, The Poser makes growth in wisdom and knowledge the first priority. Where God is envisioned as all-powerful, The Poser seeks authority over others as the way to become like God. Where God is perceived as unchanging and unconquerable, The Poser emphasizes rock-steady consistency and a high threshold for pain as the way of godliness.

The life of Jesus is a different story that suggests being like Abba means showing compassion. Donald Gray writes: "Jesus reveals in an exceptionally human life what it is to live a divine life, a compassionate life."[13] Compassion is not hard to decode. It's a compound word that combines the prefix *com*, which means "with" or "together," with the word *passion*, which means "to suffer." The two elements combine to signify *suffering together* or *suffering with* someone. The life of Jesus suggests that being Abba's Child means entering the suffering of others. And how do we do that? Read on. . . .

FORGIVENESS

> *Peter got up the nerve to ask, "Master, how many times do I forgive a brother or sister who hurts me? Seven?"*
>
> *Jesus replied, "Seven! Hardly. Try seventy times seven.*
>
> *"The kingdom of God is like a king who decided to square accounts with his servants. As he got under way, one servant was brought before him who had run up a debt of a hundred thousand dollars. He couldn't pay up, so the king ordered the man, along with his wife, children, and goods, to be auctioned off at the slave market.*
>
> *"The poor wretch threw himself at the king's feet and begged, 'Give me a chance and I'll pay it all back.' Touched by his plea, the king let him off, erasing the debt.*
>
> *"The servant was no sooner out of the room when he came upon one of his fellow servants who owed him ten dollars. He seized him by the throat and demanded, 'Pay up. Now!'*

"The poor wretch threw himself down and begged, 'Give me a chance and I'll pay it all back.' But he wouldn't do it. He had him arrested and put in jail until the debt was paid. When the other servants saw this going on, they were outraged and brought a detailed report to the king.

"The king summoned the man and said, 'You evil servant! I forgave your entire debt when you begged me for mercy. Shouldn't you be compelled to be merciful to your fellow servant who asked for mercy?' The king was furious and put the screws to the man until he paid back his entire debt. And that's exactly what my Father in heaven is going to do to each one of you who doesn't forgive unconditionally anyone who asks for mercy."[14]

The Bible draws a line from compassion to forgiveness. Abba calls his children to a lifestyle of forgiveness in a world that demands an eye for an eye. Actually, it's worse than that in a world that would just as soon see you dead as look at you, especially if you're poor or rich or gay or straight or Muslim or Hindu or Christian or a Republican or a Democrat or African or American or whatever it is about you that's different from whoever has a finger on the trigger. In the middle of that kind of crazy fear, God calls his children to love instead of hate, forgive instead of strike out. Loving God is the first commandment; loving our neighbor as we love ourselves is the second (and a whole lot like the first, Jesus says). Including people who hate us—and those we hate. Treating enemies as neighbors is the way of Christ; it's part of what marks us for the world as Abba's children.

SO IT'S COME TO THIS

Forgiven and forgiving. This is who we are: the wife whose husband forgot their wedding anniversary and the parents whose child was snuffed by a drunk driver; the victim of false accusations and the street people who live under bridges; the jilted lover and the sexually molested; elderly couples who lost their life savings to greedy thieves and the woman whose alcoholic husband squandered her inheritance; believers scandalized by blasphemous images of God and the mother in El Salvador whose daughter's tortured body was returned butchered and decomposing.

And the butchers too, bizarre as that seems. The perpetrators, the thieves and fools as well as the injured—all of us forgiven and all of us called by the power of Christ to forgive.

It seems like too much. Of course it's too much; no human can be that good without being worthless. It's too much to ask. If God knew what we know, if God faced what we face, if God . . . oh . . . wait . . . God knows. God was here and is here still—in us.

Can you believe that? It's *Mardi Gras* as I write this—Fat Tuesday—and around the world tonight people party their brains out for reasons they don't understand. But we understand. *Mardi Gras* is a symbol that got the least bit out of hand; it's a symbol of cleaning house, getting rid of everything we run to for comfort when we should/could run to the arms of our Abba.

And tomorrow the forty days of Lent begin, leading us to Easter. Lent is a symbol too. It's a symbol of admitting our failure and weakness and renewing our attempt at trusting God through thick and thin, a symbol that is easily mistaken for *being sent to our rooms to think about it*. But it's so much more than that. The ashes with which millions of Christians will mark their foreheads in a tiny cross tomorrow, at least for a few minutes, are the ashes of our sin against God and each other. These forty days and nights are about being forgiven, and what that cost Jesus, and what it costs us to unclench our fists and accept it from him over the protests of The Poser, who can't see why in the world it has to come to this.

But it does come to this, and The Poser knows it. And we know it too because God knows we'll never be able to forgive if we don't *experience* our own forgiveness.

God knows we'll never be able to forgive if we don't experience our own forgiveness.

So yes, let's go to our rooms and think about it. Sit in solitude and watch while Abba's Child dies utterly alone in bloody disgrace. Watch as he breathes forgiveness on his torturers, "Father, forgive them; they don't know what they're doing." Watch as the lights blink out, and experience the healing power of the dying Lord.

The healing of a heart is seldom an instant liberation from bitterness, anger, and hatred. More often it is a gentle growing into oneness with the One who allowed himself to be slaughtered on the way to becoming our hope and peace for this life and the next. Healing may take considerable time if the pain is buried deep. But it *will* happen. The murdered Christ is not just a heroic example: He is the power and wisdom of God, a living force in his present risenness, renovating our lives and enabling us to extend forgiveness to our enemies as he forgave us when we were his enemies.

OBVIOUS ≠ TRUE

Understanding triggers the compassion that makes forgiveness possible. Stephen Covey recalled a Sunday morning incident on the New York City subway. The few passengers aboard were browsing newspapers or dozing. Covey was engrossed in reading when a man with several small children boarded the train and bedlam erupted. The kids ran up and down the aisle screaming and wrestling. Their father made no attempt to intervene.

Elderly passengers shifted nervously. Covey waited patiently for the father to restore order: a gentle word of correction, a stern command, some expression of paternal authority—anything. Tension turned to frustration. Finally, Covey turned to the father and said kindly, "Sir, perhaps you could restore order here by telling your children to come back and sit down."

"I know I should do something," the man replied. "We just came from the hospital. Their mother died an hour ago. I just don't know what to do."[15]

Just when I think I know, I find out I don't know.

What seems most obvious is seldom what's really true.

What I don't know is almost always more significant than what I know.

Compassion leads to forgiveness when we understand where our enemy cries.

What I don't know is almost always more significant than what I know.

STONE HEARTS

> "I would suggest to you tonight that HIV/AIDS is a plague of
> biblical proportions and we should attack it with the same level

of commitment, zeal, money and resources that we have rightly applied toward combating international terrorism."[16]

—FRANKLIN GRAHAM

The world's poorest continent, Africa spends $40 million each day repaying old debts. As a result, many African countries spend more on debt payments than on basic education and health care. Moreover, according to the United Nations 28.1 million Africans — 1.5 million children — are infected with AIDS. And by the end of this decade, more than 25 million African children will have lost their mother or both parents to the virus.[17]

—MARK ROSS WITH LINDY WARREN

A 2001 Barna Research Group poll commissioned by World Vision revealed that evangelical Christians are significantly less likely than are non-Christians to give money for AIDS education and prevention programs worldwide. Only 3 percent of evangelicals say they plan to help with AIDS internationally, compared with 8 percent of non-Christians and 8 percent of self-described born-again Christians. Evangelicals were also the least likely to support children orphaned by AIDS.[18]

—SHERYL HENDERSON BLUNT

I mean, what is going on with the churches? It is incredible. I tell these evangelicals in the United States there are 2,300 verses of Scripture about the poor. It's the central message outside of personal redemption, the idea of dealing with the poor. And I'm asking them, where are they? Where are they on this?[19]

—U2 SINGER, BONO

Churches in the North do not feel the pain, do not smell the stench, do not see the emaciated faces of their own Christian brothers and sisters. . . . Churches in the United States should reflect theologically on the close connections between the sinner and the stigmatized and work toward a theology of reconciliation. Churches . . . commit the sin of omission when not doing more in this field.[20]

—UNITED NATIONS AIDS AGENCY OFFICIAL CALLE ALMEDAL

People say it would take an act of God to solve the AIDS emergency. But I think God is waiting for us to act.[21]

—BONO

Whenever the gospel is used to reduce the dignity of anyone created in God's image, it is not, of course, the true gospel. People who use God's name to justify prejudice, contempt, and hostility are not doing God's work; they're working for The Poser. This is not to say they are not sincere about God and the gospel. It is only to say they are sincerely wrong.

People who use God's name to justify prejudice, contempt, and hostility are not doing God's work; they're working for The Poser.

I have a part-time ministry with the Regional AIDS Interfaith Network in New Orleans. Our interdenominational team provides practical and spiritual care to people living with AIDS, including their families and friends. We assist with things like transportation, visiting, light housekeeping, and social outings. One man's comment sums up our mission: "My best friend for the last twelve years said to me, 'I just can't go through this with you. The grief is unbearable. I'm really frightened.' To him, I wasn't Gerald anymore. I wasn't his best friend. I was Gerald who has AIDS." He said, "You folks didn't even know me but you still want to be around me. I like that a lot."

I was telling this to a group of young pastors at the National Youth Workers Convention when one of them demanded: "But what should the Christian posture be toward the gay community?"

"In one of Jesus' farming parables," I replied, "he said to let the wheat and the weeds grow together. Paul caught this spirit when he wrote in 1 Corinthians, 'Stop passing judgment and wait upon the Lord's return.'[22] The sons and daughters of Abba are the most nonjudgmental people you'll ever meet. They get along brilliantly with sinners. Remember the place in Matthew where Jesus says, 'Be perfect as your heavenly Father is perfect'? In Luke, the same verse is translated, 'Be compassionate as your heavenly Father is compassionate.' Biblical scholars say that the two words, *perfect* and *compassionate*, can be reduced to the same reality. That means following Jesus in his ministry of compassion precisely defines the biblical meaning of being perfect as the heavenly Father is perfect.

"Besides," I continued, "I'm reluctant to push God off his judgment seat when I have neither the knowledge nor the authority to judge anyone. No one at this table has ever seen a motive. How can we know what inspired another person's action? Remember Paul's words after his discourse on homosexuality in Romans 1. He begins chapter 2, 'If you think that leaves you on the high ground where you can point your finger at others, think again. Every time you criticize someone, you condemn yourself. It takes one to know one.' I'm reminded of the line from the novelist Leo Tolstoy: 'If the sexual fantasies of the average person were exposed to view, the world would be horrified.'

"Homophobia is among the most shameful scandals of my lifetime. As one century turns to the next, it's frightening to see the intolerant moralizing from people who insist on acting holier than God. Alan Jones said, 'It is precisely among those who take their spiritual life seriously that the greatest danger lies.'[23] Religious people are as easily taken in by the tyranny of homophobia and racism as anyone else—maybe more."

Stone hearts become warm flesh when we learn where the outcast weeps—and not a minute sooner.

Stone hearts become warm flesh when we learn where the outcast weeps — and not a minute sooner.

THE OTHER IS OURSELF

Being Abba's Child is not an abstract concept for me. It's the core truth of my existence. Living in the wisdom of accepted tenderness alters my perception of reality and the way I respond to people and their life situations. How I treat my brothers and sisters every day, whether they be Caucasian, African, Asian, or Latino; how I react to the burnout on the street; how I respond to interruptions from people I don't like; how I deal with ordinary people in their ordinary unbelief on an ordinary day speaks the truth of who I am more clearly than the pro-life or antiwar sticker on the bumper of my car.

We don't protect life just to ward off death. We are sons and daughters of the High King, and we are maturing in his tenderness to the extent that we are not against but *for* others—all others—so that no human flesh is strange to us. To the extent that we can touch the hand of another in love. To the extent that for us there are no "others."

This is the work of a lifetime. It's the long, gradual process of becoming like Christ in the way I think, speak, and live each day. It is, as Henri Nouwen put it, "pulling the truth revealed to me from above down into the ordinariness of what I am, in fact, thinking of, talking about, and doing from hour to hour."[24]

Our way of being in the world is the way of tenderness. Everything else is illusion, misperception, falsehood. I can't even count the betrayals and infidelities I've perpetrated in this lifetime. But I still cling to the illusion that I and my associates must be morally flawless and without human weakness. Every time I allow anything but compassion to drive me—self-righteous anger, moralizing, defensiveness, this urge to be in other people's business, criticism, frustration at people's blindness, spiritual superiority, self-justification—every time I go there, I'm alienated from my true identity as Abba's Child. And I drive a wedge between me and the people I'm supposed to love with the love of Christ.

The compassionate life is neither sloppy goodwill nor the plague that Robert Wicks calls "chronic niceness." It does not insist that a widow become friendly with her husband's murderer. It does not demand that we like everyone. It does not welcome sin or stand still for injustice. Compassion does not accept everything as equal—love and lust, Christian faith and atheism, tyranny and democracy. The way of tenderness avoids blind fanaticism and works to see the world with penetrating clarity. Yet the compassion of God opens our eyes to the unique worth of every person. "The other is 'ourself'; and we must love him in his sin as we were loved in our sin."[25]

BROKENNESS OWNED

Beginning in childhood, prejudice, bigotry, false beliefs, racism, and homophobic feelings and attitudes have been written on the hard drive in my head—right alongside orthodox Christian beliefs. They are all defense mechanisms against loving.

I grew up in a lily-white neighborhood in Brooklyn where our language routinely included "nigger, spic, kike, wop, sheeny, faggot, swish, and queer." In 1947 when Branch Rickey, president of our beloved

Brooklyn Dodgers, broke the color line by inviting Jackie Robinson to play in the major leagues, we called him a nigger-lover and many of us switched our allegiance to the New York Yankees. We were particularly annoyed by educated, assertive black men like Malcolm X, a person who clearly did not know his place and whose voice rose in what I felt was unjustifiable anger as he challenged white supremacy in the face of black beauty, black need, and black excellence. Irish Catholics like me spoke a language of stereotypes that whips up fear, ignorance, and votes and keeps genuine dialogue to a minimum.

The infections of racism and homophobia from my childhood have not vanished through intellectual enlightenment and spiritual maturity. They are still in me, as complex and deep as my blood and bones. I have carried them all my life with varying degrees of awareness but always carefully, always with the most delicate attention to the pain I would feel if I were somehow forced to acknowledge them. I have tried to deny, ignore, and repress racist and homophobic prejudices as utterly unworthy of a minister of the gospel. I feared that acknowledging their existence would give them power. Ironically, denial and repression turn out to be what gives them power. These days I am increasingly aware of the opposite compulsion. I want to know as fully and exactly as I can how deep the infection goes and what it's doing to me. And I want to be healed. I want to be free of the infection myself, and I don't want to pass it on to my children.[26]

The Poser shrinks only when he is acknowledged and accepted as an embarrassing but very real part of me. The self-acceptance that comes from embracing my core identity as Abba's Child enables me to face my utter brokenness with ruthless honesty and complete trust in the God of mercy. As my friend Sister Barbara Fiand said, "Wholeness is brokenness owned and thereby healed."

The Poser shrinks only when he is acknowledged and accepted as an embarrassing but very real part of me.

TAKE A LOOK AT A ROSE

I think homophobia and racism are among the most polarizing and distressing moral issues of this generation.

The anything-goes passiveness of the religious and political Left is matched by the preachy moralism of the religious and political Right. The person who uncritically embraces any party line is guilty of an idolatrous surrender of her core identity as Abba's Child. Neither liberal fairy dust nor conservative hardball addresses our ragged human dignity.

Abba's children seek a third option, guided first of all by God's Word. All religious and political systems, Right as much as Left, are the work of human beings. Abba's children will not sell out to conservatives or liberals. They cling to their freedom in Christ to live the gospel—uncontaminated by cultural dreck, political debris, and the fancy footwork of bullying religion. Those who are bent on handing gays over to the torturers can lay no claim to moral authority over Abba's children. Jesus said people like that corrupt the heart of true spirituality, turning Eden into a vacant lot, a wasteland, a bomb crater; creating a church where people endure lonely spiritual alienation from their best human instincts.

Frederick Buechner wrote, "We have always known what was wrong with us. The malice in us even at our most civilized. Our insincerity, the masks we do our real business behind. The envy, the way other people's luck can sting us like wasps. And all the slander, making such caricatures of each other that we treat each other like caricatures, even when we love each other. All this infantile nonsense and ugliness. 'Put it away,' Peter says. 'Grow up to salvation. For Christ's sake, grow up.'"[27]

That's what we're talking about—growing up! The command of Jesus to love each other is never limited by the nationality, status, ethnic background, sexual preference, or inherent lovability of the "other." The other, who has a claim on my love, is anyone to whom I am able to respond, as the parable of the good Samaritan makes plain:

> *What do you think? Which of the three became a neighbor to the man attacked by robbers?"*
>
> *"The one who treated him kindly," the religion scholar responded.*
>
> *Jesus said, "Go and do the same."*[28]

This insistence on the absolutely indiscriminate nature of compassion within the kingdom of God is the dominant perspective of almost all of Jesus' teaching. What is indiscriminate compassion?

> *Take a look at a rose. Is it possible for the rose to say, "I'll offer my fragrance to good people and withhold it from bad people"? Or can you imagine a lamp that withholds its rays from a wicked person who seeks to walk in its light? It could do that only by ceasing to be a lamp. And observe how helplessly and indiscriminately a tree gives its shade to everyone, good and bad, young and old, high and low, to animals and humans and every living creature—even to the one who seeks to cut it down. This is the first quality of compassion—its indiscriminate character.*[29]

NO LABELS

I took a day off with my wife to play in the French Quarter in New Orleans. We wandered around Jackson Square sampling gumbo and jambalaya, and finally stopped at the Häagen-Dazs shrine for the big finish: a praline-pecan Creole hot-fudge sundae — a religious experience in a bowl.

As we rounded the corner at Bourbon Street, a smiling girl, around twenty-one years old, approached us, pinned flowers on our jackets, and asked if we would like to make a donation to support her mission. When I inquired what her mission was, she replied, "The Unification Church."

"Your founder is Doctor Sun Myung Moon, so I guess that means you're a Moonie?"

"Yes," she answered.

She had two strikes against her in my book. She was a pagan who didn't acknowledge Jesus Christ as her Lord and Savior. And she was a witless, naive kid who had been mesmerized by a cult. "You know something, Susan?" I said. "I deeply admire your integrity and your faithfulness to your conscience. You're out here tramping the streets doing what you really believe in. You are a challenge to anyone who claims the name 'Christian.'" My wife reached out and embraced her, and I embraced the two of them.

"Are you Christians?" she asked. We nodded.

She lowered her head and we saw tears falling on the sidewalk. A minute later she said, "I've been on my mission here in the Quarter for eight days now. You're the first Christians who have ever been nice to me. The others have either looked at me with contempt or screamed and told me that I was possessed by a demon. One woman hit me with her Bible."

You wanna know what gets people's attention? Fear and hope. We know what fear does—fear of failing, looking foolish, being left out, abandoned, ignored. Fear flashes a distress signal into the night that summons The Poser to our rescue—which, of course, turns out to be no rescue at all.

Hope, on the other hand, is nurtured by the gentle hands of compassion: the way of tenderness that knows no borders, no labels, no isolation, no bigoted divisions. Christian faith is consumed with hope for what may yet be by the grace of God. Jesus, the human Face of God, brings hope wherever he comes. Hope is the way of true discipleship; the radically different mindset of Abba's children.

Hope is the way of true discipleship; the radically different mindset of Abba's children.

HOLIER THAN GOD

> *The intolerance that has spread over the world with the advent*
> *of Christianity is one of its most curious features.*[1]
>
> —BERTRAND RUSSELL IN *WHY I AM NOT A CHRISTIAN*

It doesn't take a genius to see that religious people tend to be more narrow than broad. History tells that story, and if Bertrand Russell was right, people who practice the Christian religion are among the worst offenders. He's certainly not alone in that opinion; ask around.

Instead of expanding our capacity for life, joy, and mystery, religion generally shrinks it. As systematic theologies grow, the sense of wonder dies. Religious thinkers find ways to solve the puzzles, contradictions, and uncertainties — they figure God out. Ideas and words replace encounters with God. The history of the Creator pursuing his lost creation down the corridors of time to perform a death-defying rescue gets trivialized into God's little instruction book for a happy life. *Mystery? No thanks, we've got proof! Faith? Not necessary, we have certainty!*

Of course you do.

WHO'S IT GONNA BE?

This is not the only time this has happened. Jesus was constantly in the face of a group of Jewish fundamentalists called the Pharisees — *the Separated Ones.* At the risk of oversimplifying, the Pharisees originated within Jewish culture in the four hundred years between Malachi and

Matthew. They claimed their teachers were the only ones who truly understood the Bible and, therefore, the only ones who really understood G-D. So they were strict about pretty much everything—especially the Jewish *Sabbath*.

Sabbath means *rest* and, from the beginning, the Sabbath was first and foremost God's own celebration of his creative work. Here's part of the story in Genesis:

> *God looked over everything he had made;*
> > *it was so good, so very good!*
> *It was evening, it was morning—*
> *Day Six.*
> *Heaven and Earth were finished,*
> > *down to the last detail.*
> *By the seventh day*
> > *God had finished his work.*
> *On the seventh day*
> > *he rested from all his work.*
> *God blessed the seventh day.*
> > *He made it a Holy Day*
> *Because on that day he rested from his work,*
> > *all the creating God had done.*[2]

The first time the word *Sabbath* appears in the Bible is in the story of the *manna* God sent to feed his people in the desert (how they got there is an amazing tale that begins in Genesis 37 and continues through Exodus). Just so you know, they were in the habit of counting their days from sunset to sunset for reasons that are not entirely clear. Anyway, five mornings a week (Sunday through Thursday), the people gathered a sweet, white, flaky substance that appeared overnight on the desert floor, took it home, and made bread from it. They called the substance *manna* (which means, comically, "what-is-it?"). On Friday mornings they collected enough for two days. On Saturday there was no manna on the ground because it was a day for rest — a holy Sabbath to God.[3]

The Sabbath became a celebration of God's faithfulness, a weekly exercise in doing nothing for a whole day in order to affirm that God provides for his people, even when they're wandering in the desert. The Sabbath was an act of worship and thanksgiving and faith.

When Moses declared God's Law to the people, one of the commandments went like this:

> *Observe the Sabbath day, to keep it holy. Work six days and do everything you need to do. But the seventh day is a Sabbath to GOD, your God. Don't do any work — not you, nor your son, nor your daughter, nor your servant, nor your maid, nor your animals, not even the foreign guest visiting in your town. For in six days GOD made Heaven, Earth, and sea, and everything in them; he rested on the seventh day. Therefore GOD blessed the Sabbath day; he set it apart as a holy day.*[4]

Resting from the preoccupation with making and maintaining a living was a reality check: Someone's in control and it isn't any of us, okay? So just relax and stop trying to run the world.

Time passes, God is faithful, people do dumb stuff anyway, and Exodus 31 ups the stakes by quite a bit:

> GOD spoke to Moses: "Tell the Israelites, 'Above all, keep my
> Sabbaths, the sign between me and you, generation after gener-
> ation, to keep the knowledge alive that I am the GOD who
> makes you holy. Keep the Sabbath; it's holy to you. Whoever
> profanes it will most certainly be put to death. Whoever works
> on it will be excommunicated from the people. There are six
> days for work but the seventh day is Sabbath, pure rest, holy
> to GOD. Anyone who works on the Sabbath will most cer-
> tainly be put to death.'"[5]

That's serious business. Had there been much water in the desert, a lot
of it would have flowed under the bridge between the first command to
rest in Exodus 16 and this stern restatement of the concept in Exodus 31.
It's as if God were saying, *"Let me make myself perfectly clear: The Sabbath is
a regular sign of your intentions toward me. You can only worship one of us — you
or me? What's it gonna be? Will you acknowledge me as your provider, or do you
plan to grab the credit for yourself? Are you going to trust me or yourself? I really
mean this. Take your time; I'll wait for your answer till, say, Friday at sundown."*

HISSY FITS

Fast forward to the prophet Isaiah, who speaks of the Sabbath as "a day
of joy."

> If you watch your step on the Sabbath
>   and don't use my holy day for personal advantage,
> If you treat the Sabbath as a day of joy,
>   GOD's holy day as a celebration,
> If you honor it by refusing "business as usual,"
>   making money, running here and there —
> Then you'll be free to enjoy GOD![6]

Not bad. Fasting and mourning were forbidden on the Sabbath. Fancy clothes were the uniform of the day, and joyous music was the soundtrack. And the celebration spilled out of the temple and into peoples' homes. The Sabbath was (and still is) the big event in orthodox Jewish homes — so much so that the Sabbath is considered the foundation of the tight family structure that characterized orthodox Jews through the centuries. Every member of the family was to be present for the Sabbath meal along with invited guests — especially poor people, aliens, and travelers.[7]

The Sabbath celebration started at sundown on Friday with the mother of the family lighting the ceremonial candles. Then the father, after saying grace over a cup of wine, laid his hand on the head of each of his children and blessed them with a personal prayer. The Sabbath celebration turned Jewish homes into little sanctuaries where the parents were the priests and the family table was the altar. It was a beautiful thing.

Sadly, the horrors of the Babylonian exile[8] prompted a segment of Jewish leaders to flip out on the subject of God's laws. After all, it was the nation's disobedience that made God mad enough to send them into slavery in Babylon. So it only made sense to get compulsive about avoiding anything that might possibly be construed as the tiniest bit disobedient, right?

This segment, who came to be called Pharisees, lost sight of the Sabbath's primary meaning. They hijacked the Day of God's Rest and turned it into a set of cold, legalistic requirements — mainly *thou-shalt-nots*. They ended up with a false image of God as the eternal, small-minded bookkeeper who is only happy when people pay close attention to things like how many steps a person is allowed to walk on the Sabbath. In their hands, religion became a weapon to intimidate and enslave rather than liberate and empower. Jewish believers were instructed to focus their attention not so much on worshiping and trusting God as on showing how good they were by not going to work on the Sabbath.

Their teaching was a betrayal of God's kindness. T. S. Eliot put his finger on it:

> *The last temptation is the greatest treason:*
> *To do the right deed for the wrong reason.*[9]

The joyful celebration of God's creation and faithfulness disappeared in a cloud of legalism. The means became the end. Rest became work. God's reliability was replaced by human responsibility for rules that have nothing to do with resting in God's amazing kindness.

And then, in the fullness of time, Jesus was born. And everything changed.

Jesus was not impressed with the Pharisees' Sabbath—not impressed at all—which just launched them into murderous hissy fits.

A FLEXIBLE HEART

Everything changed when Jesus came among us. But not everything stayed changed. The word *pharisee* became synonymous with *hypocrite* and—hard to believe—Christian faith mutated into Christian religion and grew its own crop of Pharisees, though they would never, ever call themselves that for obvious reasons.

Here's the funny thing: History tells us it's not whores, thieves, and pagans who find it most difficult to turn from self-reliance; it's devoutly religious Pharisees who feel they have nothing to turn from. A little goodness goes a long way toward separating a self-righteous man from God's tender mercies. It's always been like this.

A little goodness goes a long way toward separating a self-righteous man from God's tender mercies.

Pharisees invest heavily in religious gestures, rituals, methods, and techniques. "Do it just this way," they tell their followers and breed supposedly holy disciples who are judgmental, mechanical, lifeless, afraid, and as intolerant of others as they (secretly) are of themselves. They're violent people, the very opposite of holiness and love. Jesus did not die at the hands of muggers, rapists, or thugs. He fell into the well-scrubbed hands of deeply religious, totally respectable members of society.

> *One Sabbath, Jesus was strolling with his disciples through a field of ripe grain. Hungry, the disciples were pulling off the heads of grain and munching on them. Some Pharisees reported them to Jesus: "Your disciples are breaking the Sabbath rules!"*
>
> *Jesus said, "Really? Didn't you ever read what David and his companions did when they were hungry, how they entered the sanctuary and ate fresh bread off the altar, bread that no one but priests were allowed to eat? And didn't you ever read in God's Law that priests carrying out their Temple duties break Sabbath rules all the time and it's not held against them?*
>
> *"There is far more at stake here than religion. If you had any idea what this Scripture meant — 'I prefer a flexible heart to an inflexible ritual' — you wouldn't be nitpicking like this. The Son of Man is no lackey to the Sabbath; he's in charge."*[10]

The stakes are not small here. The Pharisees insist on the overriding importance of the rule of law. The dignity and needs of human beings are irrelevant. And here is Jesus, insisting law is not an end in itself but the means to an end: Obeying God expresses our love for God and our neighbors, so any religious act that stands in the way of true love stands in the way of the true God. "I prefer a flexible heart to an inflexible ritual."

The Pharisees did not take this news well.

> *When Jesus left the field, he entered their meeting place. There was a man there with a crippled hand. They said to Jesus, "Is it legal to heal on the Sabbath?" They were baiting him.*
>
> *He replied, "Is there a person here who, finding one of your lambs fallen into a ravine, wouldn't, even though it was a Sabbath, pull it out? Surely kindness to people is as legal as kindness to animals!" Then he said to the man, "Hold out your hand." He held it out and it was healed. The Pharisees walked out furious, sputtering about how they were going to ruin Jesus.*[11]

People like that don't like to be challenged. They take it personally, but they act and talk as if it were God they were defending. Jesus put them (as he always puts The Poser) in a bad spot. He'd already said he came to fulfill the Law, not destroy it. Now he made it obvious that, as far as he was concerned, the Pharisees' laws were not the same as God's Law at all.

The Pharisees' spirit lives today in those who use religion to control and humiliate others, entangling them in spools of religious red tape, watching them struggle with impossible demands and overwhelming guilt but failing to point them to the God who gives manna to the hungry and rest to the weary. The person who recently hung the

"Homosexuals are not welcome" sign on a Western church is not much different from the one who posted the "No dogs or niggers!" sign in a southern thrift store in the 1940s. Both are saying they're better than someone else for whom Jesus died. This is not the way of Jesus who, by the way, is on the record about preferring a flexible heart.

NO HUGGING

"Whoever in history has put the law, the regulation, the tradition ahead of the suffering person," Eugene Kennedy claims, "stands in the same field of grain [as the Pharisees] smugly making the same accusation against the innocent."[12] Do you have any idea how many lives have been ruined in the name of narrow-minded, intolerant religiosity? Me either. But we know the Pharisee's specialty in every age is blaming, accusing, and guilt-tripping others. This is his signature, his most reliable response to anyone who doesn't toe the line.

On my way to a funeral one day, I drove over a bridge observing the 55-miles-per-hour limit. When I spotted a sign ahead restoring the speed limit to 65, I quickly accelerated to 70 and was abruptly flagged down by a policeman. The officer was black. I explained that I was hurrying to a funeral. He listened with indifference, checked my license, and wrote me a stiff speeding ticket. In my mind I immediately accused him of racism and vindictiveness, and blamed him for my late arrival at the church.

Omagosh! What just happened there? My sleepy inner Pharisee woke up and announced he was alive and well.

Shifting blame is a defensive substitute for honest self-examination. Heaven forbid I should look for personal growth in response to my failure. *No way*, The Poser advises; *it's somebody else's fault.* We end up like the characters on *Seinfeld,* whose creators determined there would be no hugging and no learning. Period.

Shifting blame is a defensive substitute for honest self-examination.

AN IMPOSSIBLE BURDEN

The attitude of the Pharisee — then and now — is that keeping the Law obligates God. The Pharisee isn't looking for any favors; he just wants what's coming to him because he earned it. Jesus turns that upside down. Being accepted, captivated, and loved by God comes first, and that's what motivates the disciple to live out the law of love. "First we were loved, now we love. He loved us first."[13]

Suppose a child has never experienced any love from her parents. One day she meets another little girl whose parents shower her with affection. The first child says to herself: "I want to be loved like that too. I'm going to do whatever it takes to earn the love of my mother and father." So to gain the affection of her parents, she brushes her teeth, makes her bed, smiles, minds her manners, never whines or cries, never expresses a need, and learns to conceal her negative feelings.

This is the way of Pharisees. They follow the Law flawlessly in order to provoke God's love. Where necessary, they rewrite the Law to emphasize things they weren't planning to do anyway: No Dancing Allowed; No Smoking; No Drinking. Or things they prefer: Commitment to Church Programs Equals Commitment to God; Voting (*Write Your Political Affiliation Here*) Is What Jesus Would Do. Their image of God locks them into a theology of working in exchange for approval from on high. If God is the meticulous bookkeeper, eager to find fault with anybody and everybody, the Pharisee must pursue a lifestyle that minimizes mistakes. Then, on Judgment Day, he can present God with a perfect slate and God will be bound to accept it.

What an impossible burden! The ordeal of making oneself presentable to a distant, perfectionist God is exhausting. Legalists can never live up to the expectations they project on God because, as Kennedy reminds us, "There will always be a new law, and with it a new interpretation, a fresh hair to be split by the keenest ecclesiastical razor."[14] This is one way new churches, denominations, and Christian organizations are born: Two Pharisees face off and realize this town ain't big enough for both of them.

The Pharisee within is the religious face of The Poser, who always feels uneasy about his relationship with God. The compulsion to feel safe with God fuels a neurotic desire for perfection and an endless moralistic self-evaluation that makes it impossible to experience acceptance. The Poser lives under a cloud of personal failure, poor self-esteem, anxiety, fear, and depression. Other than that, it's all good. Just ask him.

The Pharisee within is the religious face of The Poser, who always feels uneasy about his relationship with God.

The Pharisee overpowers my true self whenever I choose appearance over reality, whenever I am afraid of God, whenever I surrender control of my soul to a list of rules rather than risk the uncertainty of living in union with Jesus whom I cannot see or hear.

DON'T BE LIKE ME

"If I have a message to my contemporaries," Thomas Merton said, "it is surely this: be anything you like, be madmen, drunks, . . . but at all costs avoid one thing: 'success.'"[15]

Of course Merton was referring to the cult of success, the Pharisee's fascination with honor and power, the ceaseless drive to improve The Poser's image. On the other hand, when false humility snuffs the pleasure of honest achievement and snubs genuine compliments, I become proud of my humility, alienated from real people, and The Poser rides again!

My resident Pharisee's act is never more flagrant than when I claim the high moral ground over racists, bigots, and homophobes; when I nod approvingly as the preacher trashes unbelievers, liberals, new agers, and everybody else outside the fold; when I cheer the pastor's self-confident condemnation of Hollywood movies, commercial television, the Swimsuit Issue, and all things hip-hop. I know an easy target when I see one.

Yet my library is filled with biblical commentaries and theology books. I attend church regularly and pray daily. I have a crucifix in my home and a cross in my pocket. My life is completely formed and permeated by religion. I abstain from meat on Friday. I give money to Christian organizations. I am an evangelist devoted to God and church.

> "You're hopeless, you religion scholars and Pharisees! Frauds!
> You keep meticulous account books, tithing on every nickel and
> dime you get, but on the meat of God's Law, things like fairness
> and compassion and commitment—the absolute basics!—
> you carelessly take it or leave it. Careful bookkeeping is com-
> mendable, but the basics are required. Do you have any idea
> how silly you look, writing a life story that's wrong from start
> to finish, nitpicking over commas and semicolons?
>
> "You're hopeless, you religion scholars and Pharisees!
> Frauds! You burnish the surface of your cups and bowls so

they sparkle in the sun, while the insides are maggoty with your greed and gluttony. Stupid Pharisee! Scour the insides, and then the gleaming surface will mean something.

"You're hopeless, you religion scholars and Pharisees! Frauds! You're like manicured grave plots, grass clipped and the flowers bright, but six feet down it's all rotting bones and worm-eaten flesh. People look at you and think you're saints, but beneath the skin you're total frauds."[16]

That would be me Jesus is describing. Left to myself, that would be me.

In the story of the Pharisee and the Tax Man, the Pharisee stands in the temple and prays: "Oh, God, I thank you that I am not like other people—robbers, crooks, adulterers, or, heaven forbid, like this tax man. I fast twice a week and tithe on all my income."[17]

His prayer reveals the two telltale flaws of the Pharisee. First, he is very conscious of his personal holiness. He prays in order to compare himself favorably to others, not to admit any failure or need. His fault is he believes he's faultless. There's no one he admires more. His second flaw is related to the first: the Pharisee despises others. He judges and condemns others because he's convinced he's better than they are. He's a self-righteous man who unrighteously condemns others.

In Jesus' story, the Pharisee pardons himself but is condemned by God. And the tax man condemns himself but is pardoned by God. It's a cautionary tale. One guy says, "Be like me, kids." The other guy is so humiliated by his failure he can't even make eye contact. "Don't be like me," he says in a teary whisper. And the Storyteller, with a knowing look, nods toward the tax man and mouths the words, "Be like him."

I was at a prayer meeting where a man in his mid-sixties said: "I just want to thank God that I have nothing to repent of today." His wife groaned. What he meant was he had not embezzled, blasphemed, fornicated, or recently fractured any of the Ten Commandments. He had kept himself from drunkenness, sexual irresponsibility, and outright idolatry, but he had not yet broken through to what Paul calls the inner freedom of the children of God.

We can't grow deep if we ignore the tension between the inner Pharisee, who is holier than God if you judge by who sticks closest to the rules, and Abba's Child, whose only hope of holiness comes from God's mercy. They're both in there. We get to choose which we'll nurture to full strength.

ARE YOU FEELING THIS?

In contrast to the Pharisee's perception of God and religion, the biblical writers look at the gospel like a child who has never experienced anything but love. She does her best because she is loved, and when she fails, the fear that her parents might stop loving her never enters her mind. They may disapprove of her behavior and they will certainly help her learn and grow and do better, but their love does not depend on her performance.

If the Pharisee is the religious face of The Poser, Abba's Child is the religious face of the true self. For the Pharisee, the emphasis is always on personal effort and achievement. Abba's Child rests and delights in the relentless tenderness of God.

Here's what Therese of Lisieux said about remaining a little child before the good God:

It is recognizing one's nothingness, expecting everything from the good God, just as a little child expects everything from its father; it is not getting anxious about anything, not trying to make one's fortune. . . . Being little is also not attributing to oneself the virtues that one practices, as if one believed oneself capable of achieving something, but recognizing that the good God puts this treasure into the hands of his little child for it to make use of it whenever it needs to; but it is always the good God's treasure. Finally it is never being disheartened by one's faults, because children often fall, but they are too little to do themselves much harm. [18]

Good parents love a little one before that child makes a mark on the world. A loving mother never holds up her infant to a visiting neighbor with the words, "This is my daughter. She's going to be a lawyer." So the secure child's accomplishments later in life are not an effort to gain acceptance and approval. They are the rich overflow of being loved.

Abba's Child is aware of her feelings and uninhibited about expressing them; the Pharisee edits every emotion with an automated response. The question is not whether I am an introvert or an extrovert. The issue is whether I choose to feel or crush my genuine emotions. John Powell said if he wrote the epitaph on his parents' tombstone, he would have been compelled to write, sadly: "Here lie two people who never knew one another." To open yourself to another person, to stop lying about your loneliness and fear, to be honest about what you love, to tell others how much they mean to you—this openness is the triumph of Abba's Child over the Pharisee.

Abba's Child is aware of her feelings and uninhibited about expressing them.

To ignore, repress, or dismiss our feelings is to fail to listen to the stirrings of the Spirit within our emotional life.[19] Jesus listened. In John's gospel we see Jesus wracked by the deepest emotions over the death of a friend (see 11:33). In Matthew we see his anger erupt: "Frauds! Isaiah's prophecy of you hit the bull's-eye: These people make a big show of saying the right thing, but their heart isn't in it" (15:7-9). He felt deeply for ordinary people: "When he looked out over the crowds, his heart broke. So confused and aimless they were, like sheep with no shepherd" (Matthew 9:36). Jesus expresses grief and frustration in Luke 19:41; irritation in Mark 14:6; frustration in Matthew 17:17; extraordinary sensitivity in Luke 8:46; outrage in John 2:16. And Luke records this brief encounter:

> Not long after that, Jesus went to the village Nain. His disciples were with him, along with quite a large crowd. As they approached the village gate, they met a funeral procession—a woman's only son was being carried out for burial. And the mother was a widow. When Jesus saw her, his heart broke. He said to her, "Don't cry." Then he went over and touched the coffin. The pallbearers stopped. He said, "Young man, I tell you: Get up." The dead son sat up and began talking. Jesus presented him to his mother.[20]

Do you think the widow's son would have been resuscitated if Jesus had repressed his heartbreak?

We have spread so many coats of whitewash over the historical Jesus that we scarcely see the glow of his presence anymore. Jesus is a man in a way that we have forgotten men can be: truthful, blunt, emotional, nonmanipulative, sensitive, compassionate—so liberated that he did not feel it unmanly to cry; so secure he could engage anyone head-on and deal with them right where they were. Underneath all our cover-up, the gospel portrait of the beloved child of Abba is a man exquisitely in touch with his emotions and uninhibited in expressing them.

SPIRITUAL FRIGHT MASKS

Did you ever hear a woman say, "I just need a few minutes to put on my face?" A Pharisee must wear his or her religious face at all times. The Pharisee's appetite for attention and admiration compels him to always present an inspiring image and avoid the risk of mistakes and missteps. Uncensored emotions spell big trouble for the Pharisee.

This is a problem. Emotions are our most direct experience of where we are in the moment. Feelings can be reliable or misleading—I've been startled by people who meant me no harm: the feeling was real but the threat was not. Feelings simply reflect what's going on inside us. We don't have to act on every emotion—in fact we shouldn't—but it's important to acknowledge and consider every emotion. What we do with our feelings determines whether we live honestly or falsely. When balanced with faith-formed intelligence, our emotions become important signals that inform our choices. Denying, displacing, and crushing feelings never helps anyone (except maybe the person in deep emotional shock who involuntarily shuts down rather than melting down).

The Pharisee in my head has devised a way to camouflage my emotions and gut my true self through a clever maneuver called "spiritualizing." Spiritualizing shields me from unwanted feelings—anger, fear, guilt—by tap dancing into religious generalizations that don't really mean anything.

I once wanted to say to a bigot, "If you don't cool it, I'm going to choke you and hang you as an ornament on my Christmas tree." These are unwelcome feelings for a man of the cloth. So, instead of speaking up, I reasoned to myself: "God has led this unenlightened brother into my life, and his obnoxious manner is no doubt due to some childhood trauma. I must love him in spite of everything." (Who could argue with that? If bigots hate blacks, and I hate bigots, what's the difference?) But the plain truth is, I covered up my feelings with holy-sounding nonsense. I divorced my true self and responded like a disembodied phantom (which is to say, as if I weren't there at all).

I've done it a thousand times. When a friend said, "I really don't like you anymore. You never listen to me and always make me feel inferior," I didn't grieve. I turned quickly from my heartache and concluded, "This is God's way of testing me." When money is scarce and I feel anxious, I remind myself: "Jesus said, 'don't be anxious about tomorrow,' so this little setback is just his way of finding out what I am made of." That's spiritualizing. It doesn't face the plain fact that my friendship is broken and it's my job to see if we can fix it together. Or the plain fact that I live in a world where work sometimes goes away and unexpected expenses arrive unannounced, and it's my job to surrender my anxiety to the God who cares for me. Scarcity and broken relationships aren't about God finding out what I'm made of — God knows what I'm made of — it's the other way around. In or out of friendship, in scarcity or abundance or just enough, my life is about finding out what God is made of.

If I'm not honest with myself, why in the world would I be honest with you? It's an ugly customer, this spiritualizing. It wears a thousand faces, every one of which intends to scare a little child back into hiding.

If I'm not honest with myself, why in the world would I be honest with you?

LABEL-GAZING

When my wife was a child in the tiny hamlet of Columbia, Louisiana (population 900), her weekend playmate was a little girl named Bertha Bee, the daughter of a black housekeeper named Ollie. Together, Bertha Bee and Roslyn played dolls, made mud pies by the lake, ate cookies, shared their dreams, and built castles in Spain. One Saturday Bertha Bee stopped coming to play. She never returned. Roslyn knew she wasn't sick, injured, or dead because Ollie would have told her. So Roslyn, nine years old, asked her father why Bertha Bee didn't come to play anymore. She never forgot his reply: "It is no longer appropriate," he said.

The face a child wears is her own, and her eyes looking out on the world don't strain to see labels: black-white, Catholic-Protestant, Asian-Latino, gay-straight, liberal-conservative. Label-gazing is learned behavior. Labels create impressions. This person is wealthy, that one is on welfare. This woman is brilliant, that one is dim-witted. One man is attractive, another homely. Impressions form images that become fixed ideas that harden into prejudice. Prejudice captures us in the prison of what-seems-to-be.

Anthony DeMello said, "If you are prejudiced, you will see that person from the eye of that prejudice. In other words, you will cease to see this person as a person."[21] That's how the Pharisee sees everyone, including himself. His life is all about the labels. Which gets him off the hook for listening, caring, feeling, acting for the good of another person.

FIGHT THE POWER

> *The disciples came to Jesus asking, "Who gets the highest rank in God's kingdom?"*
>
> *For an answer Jesus called over a child, whom he stood in the middle of the room, and said, "I'm telling you, once and for all, that unless you return to square one and start over like children, you're not even going to get a look at the kingdom, let alone get in. Whoever becomes simple and elemental again, like this child, will rank high in God's kingdom. What's more, when you receive the childlike on my account, it's the same as receiving me."*[22]

In the competitive game of one-upmanship, Jesus' disciples were driven by the desire for importance—they wanted to be somebody. According to John Shea, "Every time this ambition surfaces, Jesus places a child in their midst or talks about a child."[23] Jesus doesn't seem to care much for ambition.

The power games the Pharisee plays are meant to dominate people and increase his power through manipulation, control, and passive aggression. His life becomes a series of calculated moves and counter moves. The Pharisee develops a finely tuned social radar to detect and avoid people and situations that might threaten his authority.

This one-upmanship prevents the free exchange of ideas and introduces a spirit of competition that is alien to the unselfconscious child. Anthony DeMello observed, "The first quality that strikes one when one looks into the eyes of a child is its innocence; its lovely inability to lie or wear a mask or pretend to be anything other than what it is."[24]

A truly talented Pharisee can bully people and make them like it for quite a while—it's really very impressive. But the devouring Pharisee who grabs power, collects disciples, acquires knowledge, achieves status, and dominates his little world also grows fearful if an innocent underling swipes the spotlight, cynical when feedback is negative, paranoid when threatened, aggressive when challenged, and dramatic when defeated. Caught up in the power game, he lives with considerable evidence of success on the outside, but a desolate, unloving, anxiety-ridden hollowness on the inside.

The true self preserves childlike innocence through a deliberate awareness of his core identity. He refuses to be contaminated by peers whose lives, Anthony DeMello says, "are spent not in living but in courting applause and admiration; not in blissfully being themselves but in neurotically comparing and competing, striving for those empty things called success and fame even if they can be attained only at the expense of defeating, humiliating, destroying their neighbors."[25] The true self must fight the power with innocence or be overwhelmed by hollow deceit.

INTO THE FULLNESS

In this age of immense sophistication, achievement, and jaded sensibilities, the rediscovery of childhood is an engaging concept. That said, I admit I don't know you. Maybe you don't need to rediscover your inner child because she isn't lost. I hope that's true. But I doubt it. Ernest Hemingway had a character say, "The world breaks everyone," and, of course, he was right.[26] Sooner or later—usually sooner—we all do the wrong thing, or fail to do the right thing knowing good and well what we ought to do. And that's when we join the rest of the world in that sinking feeling that it's not supposed to be like this. The Doors singer

Jim Morrison's biography put it another way: it's called *No One Here Gets Out Alive*.

So if not today, then soon you'll need to recapture the little child you were for a few months or a few years, and you'll find with the rest of us that it's impossible to get back there without help. Innocence is a condition William McNamara claims "can only be enjoyed by unspoiled children, uncanonized saints, undistinguished sages and unemployed clowns."[27] Which are you?

Until we reclaim our lost child we have no inner sense of self, and gradually The Poser becomes who we really think we are. Psychologists and spiritual writers emphasize getting to know the inner child as best we can and embracing him or her as a lovable and precious part of ourselves. The positive qualities of the child—openness, trusting dependence, playfulness, simplicity, sensitivity to feelings—keep us open to fresh ideas, risky commitments, the surprises of the Spirit, and adventurous growth. The unselfconsciousness of the child keeps us from gloomy introspection, endless self-analysis, and the fatal self-absorption of spiritual perfectionism.

But we can't stop with returning home to our inner child. As Jeff Imbach noted, "If the inner child is all that is found inside, it still leaves one isolated and alone. There is no final intimacy within if all that we are reclaiming is ourselves."[28] Seeking the inner child on our spiritual journey, we discover innocence lost, but we also find what Jean Gill called "the child in shadow."[29] The shadow child is undisciplined and potentially dangerous, self-absorbed and self-willed, mischievous and capable of hurting a puppy or another child. When the prophet said, "A little child will lead them" (Isaiah 11:6), that's not who he had in mind.

Much of the shadow side of my childhood was riddled with fear. I was afraid of my parents, the church, the dark, and myself. In her novel *Saint Maybe*, Anne Tyler described Ian Bedloe like this:

> *It seemed that only Ian knew how these children felt: how scary they found every waking minute. Why, being a child at all was scary! Wasn't that what grown-ups' nightmares often reflected—the nightmare of running but getting nowhere, the nightmare of the test you hadn't studied for or the play you hadn't rehearsed? Powerlessness, outsiderness. Murmurs over your head about something everyone knows but you."*[30]

Rediscovering the inner child is not an end in itself but a doorway into the depths of our union with the God who makes himself at home in us; it's a sinking down into the fullness of the Abba experience, into the vivid awareness that my inner child is Abba's Child, held fast by him, both in light and in shadow.

Rediscovering the inner child is not an end in itself but a doorway into the depths of our union with the God who makes himself at home in us.

Frederick Buechner gets the last word:

> *We are children, perhaps, at the very moment when we know that it is as children that God loves us—not because we have deserved his love and not in spite of our undeserving; not because we try and not because we recognize the futility of our trying; but simply because he has chosen to love us. We are children because he is our father; and all our efforts, fruitful and fruitless, to do good,*

to speak truth, to understand, are the efforts of children who, for all their precocity, are children still in that before we loved him, he loved us, as children, through Jesus Christ our Lord.[31]

RESURRECTION

For centuries Christians have celebrated Easter with a greeting in which one says, "He is risen," and the other replies, "He is risen indeed!" My friend once received an alternate greeting from an old guy who wasn't paying much attention. My friend smiled and said, "He is risen!" The old man replied, "Fine thanks, and you?"

Even on Easter Sunday, people have other things on their minds. No problem; there are places to go, things to be done. But think about it a moment: He was crucified, dead, and buried. And now he is risen. Is there anything this can possibly leave untouched?

There's a story about the writer G. K. Chesterton, whose conversion to Christian faith caused quite a stir in Great Britain at a time when smart people (and Chesterton was brilliant) weren't supposed to believe. So he's standing on a street corner in London when he's approached by a newspaper reporter. "Sir, I understand that you recently became a Christian," the reporter says. "May I ask you one question?"

"Certainly," says Chesterton.

"If the risen Christ suddenly appeared at this very moment and stood behind you," the reporter inquires, "what would you do?"

And Chesterton looks the reporter square in the eye and replies, "He is."

///

At the risk of stating what's obvious, let me just say, the Resurrection is a big deal. Perhaps The Big Deal. If it's true, there's a rip in the fabric of space and time. If it's not true, I suppose we're on our own.

The Resurrection is a big deal.

The apostle Paul was talking to Christians in a culture with values a lot like ours when he wrote:

> *The first thing I did was place before you what was placed so emphatically before me: that the Messiah died for our sins, exactly as Scripture tells it; that he was buried; that he was raised from death on the third day, again exactly as Scripture says; that he presented himself alive to Peter, then to his closest followers, and later to more than five hundred of his followers all at the same time, most of them still around (although a few have since died); that he then spent time with James and the rest of those he commissioned to represent him; and that he finally presented himself alive to me.*[1]

If the Christian story is true (and I'm betting my life it is), it changes everything. If the Christian story is true, *death* is not the final word; it's *resurrection*. If the Christian story is true, what Jesus does for us *right now* is as real and fresh as what he *did* for us back in the day. This is why Paul was so forceful when he wrote,

> *Compared to the high privilege of knowing Christ Jesus as my Master, firsthand, everything I once thought I had going for me*

*is insignificant—dog dung. I've dumped it all in the trash so
that I could embrace Christ and be embraced by him. I didn't
want some petty, inferior brand of righteousness that comes from
keeping a list of rules when I could get the robust kind that
comes from trusting Christ—God's righteousness. I gave up all
that inferior stuff so I could know Christ personally, experience
his resurrection power, be a partner in his suffering, and go all
the way with him to death itself. If there was any way to get in
on the resurrection from the dead, I wanted to do it.*[2]

"If there was any way to get in on the resurrection from the dead, I
wanted to do it." Well who wouldn't?

"Does it give you comfort to know you will live on in the hearts of
your people?" *Rolling Stone* asked Woody Allen. To which he replied, "I
would rather live on in my apartment."

C. S. Lewis commented, "There are, aren't there, only three things
we can do about death; to desire it, to fear it, or to ignore it."[3]

"The one who dies with the most toys, still dies."

"If there was any way to get in on the resurrection from the dead,"
Paul said, "I wanted to do it." Me too.

DEATH IS DEAD

For me, the most radical demand of Christian faith is embracing the
resurrection of Jesus Christ every day. I've been a Christian for half a
century. My first blush of relief and joy faded into the undramatic rou-
tine of my life a long time ago. Add to that numerous bouts of egoma-
nia, followed by self-hatred and binge drinking, and maybe I haven't

always been the poster boy for Christian conduct. So embracing the Resurrection every day feels scary to me. Given what I've experienced of desolation and abandonment, and the death of my father, and the shadow of loneliness and fear, and the nagging Pharisee in my head, and the desperate Poser, it's a big deal to say the words *Christ is risen* every day—even to myself.

Oh, I think it in my head, but I don't always *believe* it all the way to the soles of my feet. And that's a troubling development for a man in my position. If I embrace the Resurrection, I'm saying I believe his power is loose in the world and loose in me too, rooting out and over-coming death wherever he finds it because death is not the last word, as Frederick Buechner says, but only the next to last.

Why is that difficult for me to believe from my head to my heels? I'm not sure; I'm working on it. Meanwhile, I'm sticking with what I think is true: Christ is alive right now and death is dead for good.

Christ is alive right now and death is dead for good.

REMEMBERING

This is a tense question—which is to say, a question of past and pres-ent tenses. It's not simply, *was* Jesus resurrected from death but *is* he res-urrected right now? Big difference.

The theologian H. A. Williams says the Resurrection must be experienced as more than a past historical event. Otherwise, he wrote, "it is robbed of its impact on the present. . . . It is remote and isolated. And that is why for the majority of people it means nothing."[4] He's saying that WAS is not IS. WAS is interesting—in that vague, historical way—but IS is *fascinating* because it means something *right now*. Jesus is resurrected from the dead and sits at the right hand of God the Father *right now.* "He's there from now to eternity to save everyone who comes to God through him, always on the job to speak up for them."[5] *Fascinating.* There's a difference between past tense and present tense.

There's also a difference between present tense and future tense. If we're not careful, our hope that Christ's resurrection will somehow lead to our own one day threatens to push the resurrected Jesus out of the present and disconnect him from what goes on day after day. Do we need resurrection in the future? Absolutely. There's no argument about that. But I want to know if resurrection matters today. Today is what we have. Today is when we can make a difference. We can respond to God today. We can serve people today. The only day we can ever live is today. The sign on the side of Joe's Crab Shack says *Free Crabs Tomorrow.* Stop on by this evening and tell them you've come in for your free crabs. They'll smile and shake their heads and say, "Oh, gee, no, sorry: that's *tomorrow.*"

Well, good news: The Resurrection is today.

On my best days, I remember the Resurrection and it changes me. In the Resurrection I find meaning in apparently disconnected and useless experiences. I have a close call on the highway and find I'm not afraid to die because I remember the Resurrection. There's not enough time for everyone to have his say and I'm afraid people will think I have nothing to contribute, but I decide to let someone else speak because I remember the Resurrection. Resurrection helps us understand that our lives are all one piece. Resurrection reveals the great design.

It is the resurrected Christ who said, "God authorized and commanded me to commission you: Go out and train everyone you meet, far and near, in this way of life, marking them by baptism in the threefold name: Father, Son, and Holy Spirit. Then instruct them in the practice of all I have commanded you. I'll be with you as you do this, day after day after day, right up to the end of the age."[6] Remembering the Resurrection helps us look beyond ourselves and stay alert for the subtle but significant presence of Christ day after day after day.

CONGRATULATIONS, MA

William Barry wrote, "We must school ourselves to pay attention to our experience of life in order to discern the touch of God or what Peter Berger calls the rumor of angels from all the other influences on our experience."[7]

Frederick Buechner describes two experiences that may be whispered rumors from the wings—or they may not be whispers from anywhere. He leaves the reader to decide.

> One of them happened when I was in a bar at an airport at an unlikely hour. I went there because I hate flying and a drink makes it easier to get on a plane. There was nobody else in the place, and there were an awful lot of empty barstools on this long bar, and I sat down at one which had, like all the rest, a little menu in front of it with the drink of the day. On the top of the menu was an object—and the object turned out to be a tie clip and the tie clip had on it the initials C.F.B., which are my initials, and I was actually stunned by it, just B would have been sort of interesting, F.B. would have been fascinating, and C.F.B., in the right order—the chances of that being a chance I should think would be absolutely astronomical. What it meant to me, what I chose to believe it meant was: You are in the right place, the right errand, the right road at that moment.

How absurd and how small, but it's too easy to say that.

And then another one was just a dream I had of a friend that recently died, a very undreamlike dream where he was simply standing in the room and I said: "How nice to see you, I've missed you," and he said, "Yes, I know that," and I said: "Are you really there?" and he said: "You bet I'm really here," and I said: "Can you prove it?" and he said "Of course I can prove it," and he threw me a little bit of blue string which I caught. It was so real that I woke up. I recounted the dream at breakfast the next morning with my wife and the widow of the man in the dream and my wife said, "My God, I saw that on the rug this morning," and I knew it wasn't there last night, and I ran up and sure enough, there was a little squibble of blue thread. Well again, either that's nothing — coincidence — or else it's just a little glimpse of the fact that maybe when we talk about the resurrection of the body, there's something to it![8]

Maybe there *is* something to it. Late one Saturday night, I returned home to a sad message on my answering machine: "Frances Brennan is dying and wants to see you."

I flew to Chicago the next day, took a cab to San Pierre, Indiana, and arrived at the Little Company of Mary nursing home around 9:00 P.M. I went to the fourth floor and asked the night nurse if Mrs. Brennan was still in her room. "Yes," she replied, "room 422, straight down the hall."

She was lying in bed, this ninety-one-year-old woman, so frail now. She'd been a second mother to me for forty years. It was her last name I took as my first name in 1960. A nun sat beside her, praying softly.

"She's been waiting for you," the sister said.

I leaned over the bed, kissed Frances on the forehead, and said, "I love you, Mom." She raised her right hand and pointed to her lips. After a few seconds of uncertainty I sensed what she wanted. With the tiny energy in her sixty-two-pound body, she pursed her lips and we kissed three times, and she smiled. She died a few hours later.

After the sun came up, I drove back to Chicago to make burial arrangements. I decided to stay on Cicero Avenue because it was close to Lamb's Funeral Home. After getting my room key, I took the elevator to the fourth floor, walked numbly down the hall, glanced at the key, and inserted it in the door. Room 422.

I don't know, I was exhausted and emotionally spent, so maybe it was an overreaction, but here's what I remember: I dropped my bag on the floor and sank into a soft chair, stunned. There were 161 rooms in the motel and I got room 422. Like a bell sounding deep in my soul, these words echoed inside me: "Why do you seek the living among the dead?" Outside the clouds broke and sunlight burst through the window. My face split into a wide grin. "You're alive, Ma! Congratulations, you're home!"

Reading the Celtic chronicles I was struck by the clear vision of faith in the medieval church of Ireland. When a young monk saw his cat catch a salmon swimming in shallow water, he cried, "The power of the Lord is in the paw of the cat." The chronicles tell of wandering sailor monks of the Atlantic seeing the angels of God and hearing their song as they rose and fell over the western islands. To the modern person they were only gulls and gannets, puffins, cormorants, and kittiwakes. "But the monks lived in a world in which everything was a word of God to them, in which the tenderness of God was manifest in accidental signs, nocturnal communiques, and the ordinary stuff of our pedestrian lives."[9] I think if the Father of Jesus monitors every sparrow that falls from the sky and every hair that drops from our heads, perhaps it is not beneath his resurrected Son to dabble in room keys, monogrammed tie clips, and squibbles of thread.

HIGH EXPLOSIVES

An amazing thing happened in Jerusalem at the Feast of Pentecost, fifty days after the Resurrection. That day, the first followers of Jesus told the world about his resurrection at the top of their lungs. They did it in a way they could not have planned. Looking back, it's not hard to see who was behind it. Starting in chapter seven, John's gospel reveals the thread that weaves toward Pentecost:

> *[Jesus] cried out, "If anyone thirsts, let him come to me and drink. Rivers of living water will brim and spill out of the depths of anyone who believes in me this way, just as the Scripture says." (He said this in regard to the Spirit, whom those who believed in him were about to receive. The Spirit had not yet been given because Jesus had not yet been glorified.)*[10]

He picks it up again twice in chapter 14:

> *"If you love me, show it by doing what I've told you. I will talk to the Father, and he'll provide you another Friend so that you will always have someone with you. This Friend is the Spirit of Truth. The godless world can't take him in because it doesn't have eyes to see him, doesn't know what to look for. But you know him already because he has been staying with you, and will even be in you!"*[11]

If you love me, show it by doing what I've told you.

> *"I'm telling you these things while I'm still living with you. The Friend, the Holy Spirit whom the Father will send at my request, will make everything plain to you. He will remind you of all the things I have told you."*[12]

There's more in chapter 15:

> *"When the Friend I plan to send you from the Father comes — the Spirit of Truth issuing from the Father — he will confirm everything about me. You, too, from your side must give your confirming evidence, since you are in this with me from the start."*[13]

And chapter 16:

> *"It's better for you that I leave. If I don't leave, the Friend won't come. But if I go, I'll send him to you.*
>
> *"When he comes, he'll expose the error of the godless world's view of sin, righteousness, and judgment: He'll show them that their refusal to believe in me is their basic sin; that righteousness comes from above, where I am with the Father, out of their sight and control; that judgment takes place as the ruler of this godless world is brought to trial and convicted.*
>
> *"I still have many things to tell you, but you can't handle them now. But when the Friend comes, the Spirit of the Truth, he will take you by the hand and guide you into all the truth there is. He won't draw attention to himself, but will make sense out of what is about to happen and, indeed, out of all that I have done and said. He will honor me; he will take from me and*

*deliver it to you. Everything the Father has is also mine. That
is why I've said, 'He takes from me and delivers to you.'"*[14]

The first chapter of the book of Acts picks up the thread after the
Resurrection:

*As they met and ate meals together, he told them that they were
on no account to leave Jerusalem but "must wait for what the
Father promised: the promise you heard from me. John baptized
in water; you will be baptized in the Holy Spirit. And soon."*

*When they were together for the last time they asked,
"Master, are you going to restore the kingdom to Israel now? Is
this the time?"*

*He told them, "You don't get to know the time. Timing is
the Father's business. What you'll get is the Holy Spirit. And
when the Holy Spirit comes on you, you will be able to be my
witnesses in Jerusalem, all over Judea and Samaria, even to the
ends of the world."*

*These were his last words. As they watched, he was taken
up and disappeared in a cloud. They stood there, staring into
the empty sky.*[15]

Now, ten days later, we come to Acts chapter 2 and the Feast of
Pentecost. Faithful people have gathered from all over the world to
commemorate the revelation of God's Law to Moses. One hundred and
twenty of Jesus' disciples are also in Jerusalem, waiting and praying as
instructed:

*When the Feast of Pentecost came, they were all together in one
place. Without warning there was a sound like a strong wind,*

gale force—no one could tell where it came from. It filled the whole building. Then, like a wildfire, the Holy Spirit spread through their ranks, and they started speaking in a number of different languages as the Spirit prompted them.

There were many Jews staying in Jerusalem just then, devout pilgrims from all over the world. When they heard the sound, they came on the run. Then when they heard, one after another, their own mother tongues being spoken, they were thunderstruck. They couldn't for the life of them figure out what was going on, and kept saying, "Aren't these all Galileans? How come we're hearing them talk in our various mother tongues?

Parthians, Medes, and Elamites;
 Visitors from Mesopotamia, Judea, and Cappadocia,
  Pontus and Asia, Phrygia and Pamphylia,
   Egypt and the parts of Libya belonging to Cyrene;
  Immigrants from Rome, both Jews and proselytes;
  Even Cretans and Arabs!

"They're speaking our languages, describing God's mighty works!"[16]

That's how the gospel of Jesus was launched—the Spirit working through ordinary people to broadcast the Resurrection story so anyone could understand it—just the way Jesus said it would happen. The story exploded in Jerusalem with three thousand converts that day. Then the story exploded out of Jerusalem and across the Mediterranean to Rome and beyond. And today, the Resurrection story is explosive still, wherever it mixes with faith and the touch of God's Spirit.

A HOLY HAND

Remembering the present tense resurrection reminds me who is behind and before and beneath all things. Remembering doesn't add anything to the power of Christ's resurrection and it doesn't take anything away if I forget. Remembering doesn't work on God; it works on me. It reminds me to rely on the power that raised Jesus from the dead no matter what The Poser says, no matter how the Pharisee nags, no matter how dangerously close the shadow of death may seem. Christ is risen. The Spirit of God is loose in the world. This changes everything.

The Spirit of God is loose in the world. This changes everything.

Early one morning, for no apparent reason, a heavy sense of gloom settled in my soul during a writing session. I stopped writing and sat down to read the early chapters of my manuscript and got so discouraged I considered abandoning the whole project. I left the house to do some business with the Department of Motor Vehicles. The office was closed. I decided I needed exercise. After jogging two miles down the river levee, a thunderstorm hurled sheets of rain, and a howling wind almost blew me into the Mississippi. I sat down in the tall grass, vaguely aware of clinging to a nail-scarred hand. I returned to the office cold and soaked and got a phone call that led to conflict. My feelings rioted—frustration, anger, resentment, fear, self-pity, depression. I repeated to myself, "I am not my feelings." No relief. I tried, "This too shall pass." It didn't.

At six that night, emotionally drained and physically spent, I plopped down in a soft chair. I began to consciously seek out his life-giving Spirit, praying the Jesus prayer, "Lord Jesus Christ, have mercy on me, a sinner." Slowly but perceptibly I woke to his presence. The loneliness continued but grew gentle, the sadness endured but felt light. Anger and resentment vanished.

A hard day? You bet. Rattled and unglued? Certainly. Unable to cope? As it turned out, no.

How does the Spirit of the resurrected Lord show himself on days like that? By energizing our willingness to stand fast, our refusal to escape into self-destructive behavior. Resurrection power enables us to confront untamed emotions, to endure the pain, to receive it, to take it on board, however severe it may be. And in the process we find we are not alone, that we can stand fast in our awareness of present tense resurrection and so become fuller, deeper, richer disciples. We not only *hold* but *expand* the boundaries of who we think we are. We come to know ourselves as bigger than we ever imagined.

Paul said, "The mystery in a nutshell is just this: Christ is in you, therefore you can look forward to sharing in God's glory. It's that simple."[17] Our true self knows that if great trials are avoided, great deeds remain undone and the possibility of growth into greatness is aborted. Pessimism and defeatism are never the fruit of the life-giving Spirit but only reveal we have forgotten that Jesus is alive right now.

A single phone call can abruptly alter the tranquil rhythm of our lives. "Your Mom was in an accident. She's in critical condition." "I hate to be the bearer of bad news but I just saw your brother in a police car — the rumor is he's selling Ecstasy."

When tragedy crashes the party and we're deaf to everything but the shriek of our own agony, when courage flies out the window and the world looks only hostile, no human word, however sincere, offers any comfort or consolation. Our minds are numb, our hearts vacant, our nerves frayed. How will we make it when the God of our lonely journey is silent?

How will we make it when the God of our lonely journey is silent?

And yet it may happen that in these most desperate trials, beyond any rational explanation, we feel a holy hand clutching ours. We are able, as Etty Hillesun, the Dutch Jew who died in Auschwitz on November 30, 1943, wrote, "to safeguard that little piece of God in ourselves"[18] and not despair. We do make it through the night, and darkness gives way to light. The tragedy radically alters the direction of our lives, but in our vulnerability and defenselessness we experience the power of Jesus in his present tense resurrection.

WE BECOME WHOLE

In Anne Tyler's novel *Saint Maybe*, Ian Bedloe's mother is the slightly too-perfect inhabitant of a slightly too-easy world. Ceaselessly flashing a pasted-on smile, she runs in six directions at once doing whatever it is she does. But after the sudden death of her oldest son, she faces a moment of deep reflection. Driving home with her husband from Sunday morning at the Church of the Second Chance, she says:

> *"Our lives have turned so makeshift and second-class, so second-string, so second-fiddle, and everything's been lost. Isn't it amazing that we keep going? That we keep on shopping for clothes and getting hungry and laughing at jokes on TV? When our oldest son is dead and gone and we'll never see him again and our life's in ruins!"*
> *"Now, sweetie," he said.*

> "We've had such extraordinary troubles," she said, "and
> somehow they've turned us ordinary. That's what's so hard to
> figure. We're not a special family anymore."
>
> "Why, sweetie, of course we're special," he said.
>
> "We've turned uncertain. We've turned into worriers."
>
> "Bee, sweetie."
>
> "Isn't it amazing?"[19]

And with that Bee gathers herself and resumes her sweetness-and-light existence. No hugs. No learning.

Treating life as a series of disconnected episodes is a deeply rooted habit in many of us. We lack *pattern recognition* — the ability to find appropriate connections between things that are subtly related. So life seems like magic to us. We don't see how one choice leads to another, how relationships are knit and how they unravel. Life seems as disjointed as *Headline News* reporting a drop in the stock market, rising flood waters in the Midwest, a foiled terrorist plot in New York, new ways to cut cancer risk, a celebrity wedding, a golf score, box office records, and two commercial breaks. The torrent of information, events, emotions, and experiences is mind-numbing. We go limp; wait for what's next. Fall, winter, spring, summer, wedding, sickness, war, birth, divorce, change, decay, random acts. Mostly none of our business.

This doesn't improve with age.

It takes a deliberate awareness of the present tense resurrection of Jesus to make lasting sense of life. Otherwise it's mainly nonsense, aimless movement, pointless relationships, meaningless preferences.

It takes a deliberate awareness of the present tense resurrection of Jesus to make lasting sense of life.

The Resurrection binds it all together. The Resurrection gives us reasons to say *yes* to one thing and *no* to another. Remembering that Jesus sits at the right hand of God the Father, looking out for us, overcomes timidity, excites courage, inflames hope. The Resurrection gives weight to the promise that God is reshaping our lives after the image of Christ. If God can raise his Son from the dead, can God not put new life in my old bones? Can he not use everything and anything, good and bad, to accomplish his purpose in me? Nothing is irrelevant. "Everything," Keifer Sutherland said in *Flatliners*, "Everything matters."

Everything that *is* comes alive in the resurrection of Christ—who, as Chesterton noted, really is standing behind us. Everything—great, small, distant, and near—has place, meaning, value. In our union with Jesus (as Augustine said, he is more intimate with us than we are with ourselves), nothing is wasted, nothing is missing. There is never a moment that does not carry eternal significance—no action that is sterile, no wasted love, no unheard prayer. Paul writes:

> *If we don't know how or what to pray, it doesn't matter. He does our praying in and for us, making prayer out of our wordless sighs, our aching groans. He knows us far better than we know ourselves, knows our pregnant condition, and keeps us present before God. That's why we can be so sure that every detail in our lives of love for God is worked into something good.*[20]

The frustrations of circumstance, of misunderstanding, of sickness, even of our own sins, do not frustrate the final fulfillment of our lives. God uses everything.

Our intentional awareness of present tense resurrection helps us become less absorbed with appearances, less inclined to change costumes as we shift from one situation to the next. So we're no longer one person at home, another with friends; one person at church, another in traffic. We don't drift rudderless on the current of experiences that seem to just happen, idly seeking distractions to pass time, barely registering emotions, blowing off genuine offenses instead of addressing them head on. Gradually we become mature individuals whose capabilities and energies are integrated. We abandon the sense that our lives are none of our business. We become whole.

CRAZY LOVE

It was his last full night together with his followers. Jesus said:

> "Don't let this throw you. You trust God, don't you? Trust me. There is plenty of room for you in my Father's home. If that weren't so, would I have told you that I'm on my way to get a room ready for you? And if I'm on my way to get your room ready, I'll come back and get you so you can live where I live. And you already know the road I'm taking."
>
> Thomas said, "Master, we have no idea where you're going. How do you expect us to know the road?"
>
> Jesus said, "I am the Road, also the Truth, also the Life. No one gets to the Father apart from me. If you really knew me, you would know my Father as well. From now on, you do know him. You've even seen him!"
>
> Philip said, "Master, show us the Father; then we'll be content."
>
> "You've been with me all this time, Philip, and you still don't understand? To see me is to see the Father."[21]

That was a shocking thing to say. It raises the stakes incredibly. If it's false, it means we have to take another look at Jesus. An ordinary man who says something like that isn't ordinary at all; he's nuts. He thinks he's God. Or he's an evil manipulator, playing outrageous head games. In any event he's not a good guy.

And what if it's true? What if to see Jesus *is* to see the Father? Then we have to take another look at God. If Jesus doesn't just *represent* God but instead, as Karl Rahner put it, "Jesus is the human face of God," then most of the world has been wrong about God most of the time. Our speculations about what sort of force or being lies behind the universe are worse than useless if there's a Creator who makes himself known through the likes of Jesus of Nazareth.

C. S. Lewis said, "Reality, in fact, is usually something you could not have guessed. That is one of the reasons I believe Christianity. It is a religion you could not have guessed."[22] For my money, the part of the story we would least have guessed is the Resurrection because that recasts Jesus from moral example into *the* Son of God, which is shocking news that brings down the world order.

Reality, in fact, is usually something you could not have guessed.

The central miracle of the gospel is not Jesus turning water to wine or walking on water or all the signs and wonders put together. The miracle of the gospel is Christ, resurrected and glorified, seated at God's right hand and living in us by his life-giving Spirit. God our Creator, "crazed and drunk with love," as Catherine of Siena has it, lives in us and we in him in the present tense resurrection of Jesus.[23]

ONE CUP OF COLD WATER

Present tense resurrection drives us to serve Jesus by serving the least of his brothers and sisters. "When he looked out over the crowds, his heart broke. So confused and aimless they were, like sheep with no shepherd."[24] What an exquisitely tender glimpse into the soul of Jesus—brokenhearted, not condemning those aimless, wandering folk. If this reveals the intentions of the Creator, I want to look deep into his eyes for the love I need, now and forever.

Whenever the Gospels report that Jesus was moved with deep emotion, they show that it led to action—physical or inner healing, deliverance or exorcism, feeding the hungry crowds or intervening in prayer. Perhaps above all, compassion moved Jesus to repair distorted images of God and lead people out of darkness into light. I'm reminded of the messianic prophecy in Isaiah:

> *Like a shepherd, he will care for his flock,*
> *gathering the lambs in his arms,*
> *Hugging them as he carries them,*
> *leading the nursing ewes to good pasture.*[25]

Jesus' compassion moved him to tell people the story of God's love. Sometimes I try to envision what my life would be like if no one had told me God's rescue story. If I were not already dead from alcoholism, I know The Poser would be running amok. As the *Big Book of Alcoholics Anonymous* says, "Self-will runs riot."

I came across a touching story by Herman Wouk from his novel *Inside, Outside*. His hero has just become *B'nai Brith*, a son of the covenant, through his extravagant *bar mitzvah* at age thirteen:

The morning after my bar mitzvah, I returned with Pop to the synagogue. What a contrast! Gloomy, silent, all but empty; down in front, Morris Elfenbein and a few old men putting on prayer shawls and phylacteries. . . .

If Pop hadn't made the effort I'd have missed the whole point. Anybody can stage a big bar mitzvah, given a bundle of money and a boy willing to put up with the drills for the sake of the wingding. The backbone of our religion — who knows, perhaps of all religions in this distracted age — is a stubborn handful in a nearly vacant house of worship, carrying it on for just one more working day; out of habit, loyalty, inertia, super-stition, sentiment, or possibly true faith; who can be sure which? My father taught me that somber truth. It has stayed with me, so that I still haul myself to synagogues on weekdays, espe-cially when it rains or snows and the minyan looks chancy.[26]

The story of God's Law is kept alive and passed on by ten stubborn old men (a minyan) in an almost deserted synagogue. However muddled their motives and however frustrated they may become by people's apa-thy and indifference, they keep telling the story in season and out because it's the key to their identity. Our impulse to tell God's rescue story comes from listening to the heartbeat of the resurrected Jesus within us. Telling the story doesn't require becoming ordained minis-ters or street corner preachers. It doesn't call for converting people by concussion, one Bible-sledgehammer blow after another. It simply means we share with others who we truly are, how we truly need Jesus, and how Jesus is bringing us into his present tense resurrection.

The Poser is likely to draw back from telling the story because he fears rejection. He's tense and anxious because he must rely on himself, and his paltry resources limit his power. He dreads failure.

The true self is not easily discouraged because the true self knows this is not about winning and losing; it's about one beggar showing another beggar where to find bread. Or perhaps it's about a person who was dead but is now alive and on a mission to show someone else where to find the door to resurrection. "I am the Vine, you are the branches," Jesus said. "Separated, you can't produce a thing."[27] The moment we acknowledge that we are powerless, we gain access to the power of present tense resurrection and are freed from anxiety over the outcome of our storytelling. After all, it's not our story—our story is part of God's story. We don't do it from guilt or ambition (those are The Poser's motives). F. M. Cornford once said, "The only reason for doing the right thing is that it is the right thing to do; all other reasons are reasons for doing something else."[28] We tell God's story simply because it is the right thing to do.

It's not our story — our story is part of God's story.

Frank Capra is best remembered for his 1946 movie *It's a Wonderful Life*. Richard Schickel describes the film as "a fantasy about a man who falls into suicidal despair because he thinks he has accomplished nothing of value. He is rescued by a guardian angel who shows him in a gloriously realized dream sequence, how miserable the lives of his town, his friends, his family would have been had he never existed to touch them with his goodness."[29]

Perhaps when all is said and done, you will have told God's story to only one other person. Good. Get yourself ready. God promises that one cup of living water passed on will not go unrewarded.

LIKE WATER TO THE SEA

I notice a tendency in myself to sink into unawareness, to hug certain experiences and relationships to myself and exclude Christ. I indulge in what someone has called "the agnosticism of inattention." The lack of personal discipline, surrender to media bombardment, shallow reading, sterile conversation, and mechanical praying—all this dims my awareness of the resurrected Christ. Just as the failure to be attentive undermines love, confidence, and intimacy in a human relationship, so inattention to the resurrected Jesus dulls the divine relationship. As the old proverb goes, "Thorns and thistles choke the unused path." I don't deny God, exactly; I just look the other way, my attention captured by something else.

I can usually tell how I'm doing by looking at how I spend my time and money and what I talk about with my friends. Sometimes I avoid looking at those things because I prefer ignorance. It's stupid, I know.

"Without discipline we can solve nothing," Scott Peck said. "With only some discipline we can solve some problems. With total discipline we can solve all problems."[30] With each passing year I am more persuaded my chief discipline is the intentional awareness of the present tense resurrection of Jesus. From this, the other disciplines flow like water to the sea. But maintaining this discipline requires something called holy desire.

HOLY DESIRE

> *Indeed, if we consider the unblushing promises of reward and the staggering nature of the rewards promised in the Gospels, it would seem that Our Lord finds our desires, not too strong, but too weak. We are halfhearted creatures, fooling about with drink and sex and ambition when infinite joy is offered us, like an ignorant child who wants to go on making mud pies in a slum because he cannot imagine what is meant by the offer of a holiday at the sea. We are far too easily pleased.*[1]

Our Lord finds our desires, not too strong, but too weak. That idea turned heads in the middle of the last century because *desire* had come to be understood primarily as *lust*, which is one of its least interesting definitions. Desire is a longing that won't go away—which can be lusty I suppose, but just as easily holy.

It's this holy desire that interests me because it's what interested Jesus. There is a remarkable story of desire in Matthew chapter 13. It goes something like this:[2]

> *Afternoon. A dusty field. A farm worker wrestles a borrowed ox and plow across the uneven ground. Another day of toil in the weary rhythm of time. The ox stops abruptly and brazenly tosses his head from side to side. The man doesn't like this ox. The next thing, it will take off like a big clumsy bird and spoil the furrows they've already cut. Stupid beast. The man whistles*

and clucks at the ox and drives his metal blade deeper than usual to brace himself against the powerful animal. The ox strides forward again and the earth turns in rough furrows until, suddenly, the man feels the plowshare grind against something hard. He pulls back sharply and clucks at the ox, who is happy enough to stop and stand. The man backs the plow out of the furrow and lays it on its side.

This is an old field and ought to be clear of stones, but he is plowing deep — deeper, he is sure, than the other workers who are only in it for the day wage. He is different that way. He has dreams. He will own property someday — not this property; it's too far from water and too sandy. The owners don't often plant this field. He wonders why they bother at all.

Well, stones don't unearth themselves. With his bare hands he furiously digs up the earth. Dirt flies everywhere. He knows most men would let it go; it's deep, why bother? He keeps digging.

Suddenly he stops. Hello! This is odd. His finger has touched not stone but rough cloth surrounding stone. The man works the dirt away. Why does someone wrap a stone and tie it with twine? He squats, slips his fingers underneath the cord, and pulls. Suddenly, the soil gives and the man finds himself rocking back on his bottom holding what he can now see is not a stone but some kind of earthenware pot, wrapped in heavy cloth.

The rotting cord breaks as he fumbles to untie it. It's been here a while. The cloth tears away, revealing a heavy but unremarkable household pot. Trembling, he pries open the wooden lid, then lets out a scream that makes the ox flinch and stamp.

The pot is filled with jewelry and coins of silver and gold. He rifles through the treasure, letting the coins, earrings, bracelets, anklets, and chains slip through his fingers. He is transfixed by the weight of it.

Suddenly, he is afraid and looks around to see if he is being watched. This is more money than he has ever seen, more jewelry than he's ever imagined—the kind of treasure people kill for.

Once he is satisfied he is alone, he slips half a dozen small coins in his pouch, then closes and wraps and heaps the dirt back over the earthen pot. He unhitches the ox and manhandles the plow to create a shallow furrow over the surface. He steps off the distance to the southern edge of the field, counting paces, retraces his steps and walks the interval to the stone fence on the western border. As long as no one moves the boundaries, he'll be able to return to the spot.

The man rehitches the plow, his heart pounding, his head throbbing with one thought: He must own this field. Whatever it costs. He must own this field and claim the treasure.

Time passes, and the man is distracted by day and sleepless at night. Where will he get the money? Is the treasure still buried? He dare not tell anyone or tip his hand in any way. After a week, caution flies out the window. He begins selling everything he owns. He gets a fair price for his hut, then rents it back. The butcher takes the sheep off his hands. He turns to relatives and friends and takes every penny they will lend. He sells the borrowed ox and plow. His wife is concerned, then outraged: "What are you doing to us?" she demands.

"I can't tell you," he says. She pleads, then threatens, then leaves with the children. The neighbors talk. "He's drinking again." "He's off his nut." "Too much sun."

The man remains resolute, unruffled, strangely joyful for a man who's lost his family and friends and what little reputation he had.

Finally, the man makes a lowball offer on the field, then settles quickly on a price so high it makes the owner shake his head. What a rube, he thinks. No wonder he never gets ahead. He'll default on the loan and I'll have the field back before the new year. He is surprised when the man pays cash.

Taking possession of the field and its treasure, the man falls to his knees in praise to God. His fortune will pay off the debt and win back his wife and build a reputation that will make people wonder if it's true he really started out as a day laborer. "Yes," he'll say, "it all started with two dumb oxes plowing a field."

WHAT MIGHT HAVE BEEN

"God's kingdom," Jesus says, "is like a treasure hidden in a field for years and then accidentally found by a trespasser. The finder is ecstatic—what a find!—and proceeds to sell everything he owns to raise money and buy that field."[3]

That is holy desire—the longing that won't go away.

That is holy desire — the longing that won't go away.

Leslie Robins, a thirty-year-old high school teacher from Fond du Lac, Wisconsin, won a lottery jackpot of $111,000,000—serious money for a school teacher. Robins immediately flew to Lakeland, Florida, to plan the next step with his fiancée, Colleen DeVries. In a newspaper interview Robins said, "The first two days we were probably more scared and intimidated than elated. Overall, things are beginning to die down enough where we are comfortable." Comfortable, yes, I imagine so.

Robins had 180 days to claim his prize. I think I would show up at the lottery office in about 180 minutes. But let's suppose for a moment that these two Wisconsin natives are rabid sports fans. It's July, so of course they're following the Milwaukee Brewers' hapless run for the American League pennant—and then the Packers season begins, and they do love Green Bay, and *hey, wouldn't it be great to get season tickets when we claim the prize!* and the next thing they know it's January and they forgot to pick up the money. Leslie and Colleen lose $3.5 million a year for twenty years. Oh well, easy come, easy go.

What? *What?* They forgot to pick up the money?

Relax; it's just my alternate version of the story. In real life, they claimed the prize and lived more or less happily ever after.

But I can't help thinking about what I've done with my treasure. I made up a blind obsession for Leslie and picked sports out of the hat. My obsession is alcohol, and I didn't make it up. I forfeited my treasure for bourbon and vodka. During those days of sour wine and withered roses when I was stashing whiskey bottles in the bathroom cabinet, the glove compartment, and the geranium pot, I hid from God in the midst of tears and under hollow laughter. All the while I knew where I could pick up my treasure.

It is one thing to discover a treasure and quite another to claim it. *Finding* the treasure may be dumb luck—or grace. Claiming the treasure is a function of desire—the holy longing that won't go away until I act with ruthless determination, sacrifice, and tenacious effort.

The smallness of our lives is largely due to our fascination with trinkets and trophies in the unreal world that is slipping away. Sex, drugs, booze, money, pleasure, power, even a little religion, all combine to dim our awareness of present tense resurrection. Religious dabbling, worldly prestige, and weekends of sedation can't conceal the terrifying absence of meaning in the church and society—nor for that matter, can fanaticism, cynicism, or indifference.

The smallness of our lives is largely due to our fascination with trinkets and trophies in the unreal world that is slipping away.

It is astonishing that, once we know there's a treasure worth losing everything to gain, we still struggle with letting go of what we have. Is it that we really think our stuff is so valuable? Or perhaps it's just too painful to sort through it all, to put a price on each item so we can sell it. How, for example, would I put a price on what The Poser did to keep me alive all those years? It's not that The Poser is a hero; he's certainly not. But he did what he knew how to do before I knew better. Remember, he's not an outsider. Far from it. The Poser is part of me, shrinking bit by bit, but still hanging in there.

Jeff Imbach says our spiritual inactivity is a refusal to go on the inward journey—a paralysis that results from choosing to protect ourselves from passion.[4] If we do not profoundly desire the treasure in our grasp, apathy and mediocrity are inevitable. Holy desire is renewed at the source, with a fresh vision of the treasure itself. Otherwise desire is downgraded to nostalgic sentimentality over what might have been.

TWO HEARTS BEAT AS ONE

A pious Jewish couple married with great love, and the love never died. Their greatest hope was to have a child so their love could walk the earth with joy.

But there were difficulties. And since they were very pious, they prayed and prayed and prayed until—along with considerable other efforts—lo and behold, the woman conceived. And laughed like Sarah laughed when she conceived Isaac. And the child leapt in her womb like John leapt in the womb of Elizabeth when Mary visited her. And nine months later a delightful boy came rumbling into the world.

They named the child Mordecai. He was rambunctious, zestful, gobbling down the days and gulping the nights. The sun and moon were his toys. He grew in years and wisdom and grace, until it was time to go to the synagogue and learn the Word of God.

The night before his studies were to begin, his parents sat Mordecai down and instructed him on the importance of God's Word. They told Mordecai that without the Word of God he would be an autumn leaf on the winter wind. He listened wide-eyed.

But the next day Mordecai never arrived at the synagogue. Instead he found himself in the woods, swimming in the lake and climbing the trees.

When he returned home that night, news of his absence had spread through the small village. Everyone knew of his shame. His parents were beside themselves. But they had no idea what to do.

So they brought in the behavior modificationists to modify Mordecai's behavior, until there was no behavior of Mordecai that was not modified. And they went to bed knowing Mordecai would go to synagogue to learn the Word of God.

And the next day Mordecai found himself in the woods again, swimming in the lake and climbing the trees.

So they called in the psychoanalysts to analyze and unblock his blockages until there were no more blockages for Mordecai to unblock.

Nevertheless, he found himself the next day swimming in the lake and climbing the trees.

Mordecai's parents grieved for their beloved son. Sorrowful and without hope.

And it happened at this same time that the Great Rabbi came to the village. He was an imposing, somewhat fearsome man, revered by all. Mordecai's parents said, "Ah! Perhaps the Rabbi." So they took Mordecai to the Rabbi and told their tale. The Rabbi bellowed, "Leave the boy with me, and I will have a talking with him."

It was bad enough that Mordecai would not go to the synagogue. But to leave their beloved son alone with this lion of a man was most unsettling. But they had come this far, and one does not easily dismiss the command of the Great Rabbi, so they left the boy and returned home to wait.

Now Mordecai stood in the hallway, and the Great Rabbi stood in his parlor. He beckoned, "Boy, come here." Trembling, Mordecai approached the great man.

"Put down your coat and pouch," the Rabbi directed, and Mordecai did.

And then the Great Rabbi picked him up and held Mordecai silently against his heart for a long time.

The Great Rabbi picked him up and held Mordecai silently against his heart for a long time.

At dusk, Mordecai's parents came to take him home. The next day Mordecai went to the synagogue to learn the Word of God. And when he was done, he went to the woods. And the words of the woods became one with the Word of God, which became one with the words of Mordecai. And he swam in the lake. And the words of the lake became one with the Word of God, which became one with the words of Mordecai. And he climbed the trees. And the words of the trees became one with the Word of God, which became one with the words of Mordecai.

And Mordecai grew up to be a great man himself. People seized by panic came to him and found peace. People who were without anybody came to him and found communion. People with no exits came to him and found a way out. And when they asked how he came to possess God's Word so powerfully, he said, "I first learned the Word of God when the Great Rabbi held me silently against his heart."[5]

///

The heart is commonly understood as the seat of emotions from which strong feelings like love and hate arise. But that's too limited. Obviously this is not all we have in mind when we sing, "Create in me a clean heart, O God, and renew a right spirit within me." It's not what Jesus meant when he said, "You're blessed when you get your inside world — your mind and heart — put right. Then you can see God in the outside world."[6] And it's not what God meant when he said: "This is the brand-new covenant that I will make with Israel when the time comes. I will put my law within them — write it on their hearts! — and be their God. And they will be my people. They will no longer go around setting up schools to teach each other about GOD. They'll know me firsthand, the dull and the bright, the smart and the slow."[7]

The heart is the deepest essence of a person. It symbolizes what's at our core. The heart of the matter is that we can know and be known only through revealing what's in our heart.

The heart is the deepest essence of a person. It symbolizes what's at our core.

When Mordecai listened to the heartbeat of the Great Rabbi, he heard more than a palpitating human organ. He entered the Rabbi's consciousness and came to know the Rabbi in a way that embraced both intellect and emotion—and transcended them. Heart spoke to heart.

Once, on a five-day silent retreat, I spent the entire time in John's gospel. Whenever a sentence caused my heart to stir, I wrote it out longhand in a journal. The first of many entries also became the last: "The disciple Jesus loved was reclining next to Jesus. . . . He leaned back on Jesus' breast."[8] I'd read most of thirteen chapters in John before this scene jumped out at me. And after I spent five days reading John's story, this is where I ended up: watching John lay his head on the heart of God. I don't think it's there for dramatic effect. I believe it models a personal encounter with Jesus that radically alters our understanding of God and what our relationship with Jesus is meant to be. God allows a young Jew, reclining in the rags of his twenty-odd years, to listen to his heartbeat! Did anyone ever see Jesus at closer range?

Clearly, John was not intimidated by his Lord and Master.

Fearing that I would miss the divinity of Jesus, for a long time I distanced myself from his humanity. My uneasiness betrays a strange hesitancy of belief. Why was it easier for me to feel awe in the distant glow of a remote Deity than intimate confidence in a personal Savior?

John leans back on the breast of Jesus, listens to the heartbeat of the Great Rabbi, and comes to know him in a way that surpasses both intellect and distant devotion.

There's a world of difference between knowing *about* someone and *knowing* him! We may know all the details—name, place of birth, family of origin, educational background, habits, appearance, mother's maiden name—but all that tells us nothing about the person who lives and loves and walks with God.

John experiences Jesus as the human face of the God who is love. And in coming to know who the Great Rabbi is, John discovers who *he* is—*the disciple Jesus loved*. Years later he wrote, "There is no room in love for fear. Well-formed love banishes fear. Since fear is crippling, a fearful life—fear of death, fear of judgment—is one not yet fully formed in love."[9]

I WANNA BE THAT GUY

The philosopher Bernard Lonergan said: "All religious experience at its roots is an experience of an unconditional and unrestricted being in love."[10]

Uncovering holy desire begins with the recovery of my true self as the Totally Loved child of Abba. This is the goal and purpose of our lives. The apostle John did not believe Jesus was the most important thing; he believed Jesus was the One Thing.

Uncovering holy desire begins with the recovery of my true self as the Totally Loved child of Abba.

I've come to believe *that* meal, leaning against the heart of Jesus, was the defining moment in John's life. Six decades after Christ's resurrection—like an old gold miner panning the stream of his memories—he recalled the events of his three-year association with Jesus. On the last page of his story, John makes a pointed reference to that holy night when it all came together: "Peter turned and saw that the disciple whom Jesus loved was following them. (This was the one who had leaned back against Jesus at the supper and had said, 'Lord, who is going to betray you?')."[11] If John were asked, "What is your primary identity, your most coherent sense of yourself?" I don't think he would reply, "I am a disciple, an apostle, an evangelist." I think he would say, "I am the one Jesus loves."

I wanna be that guy.

///

Now stand by for one of my favorite stories.[12]

A woman asked the local priest to come and pray with her father who was dying. When the priest arrived, he found the man lying in bed with his head propped up on two pillows and an empty chair beside his bed. The priest assumed that the old fellow had been informed of his visit. "I guess you were expecting me," he said.

"No, who are you?"

"I'm the new associate at your parish," the priest replied. "When I saw the empty chair, I figured you knew I was going to show up."

"Oh yeah, the chair," the man said. "Would you mind closing the door?"

Puzzled, the priest shut the door.

"I've never told anyone this, not even my daughter," said the man, "but all my life I have never known how to pray. At the Sunday Mass I used to hear the pastor talk about prayer, but it always went right over my head. Finally I said to him one day in sheer frustration, 'I get nothing out of your homilies on prayer.'

"'Here,' says my pastor reaching into the bottom drawer of his desk. 'Read this book by Hans Urs von Balthasar. He's a Swiss theologian. It's the best book on contemplative prayer in the twentieth century.'

"Well, Father," says the man, "I took the book home and tried to read it. But in the first three pages I had to look up twelve words in the dictionary. I gave the book back to my pastor, thanked him, and under my breath whispered 'for nothin'.'

"I abandoned any attempt at prayer," he continued, "until one day about four years ago my best friend said to me, 'Joe, prayer is just a simple matter of having a conversation with Jesus. Here's what I suggest. Sit down on a chair, place an empty chair in front of you, and in faith see Jesus on the chair. It's not spooky because he promised, "I'll be with you always." Then just speak to him and listen in the same way you're doing with me right now.'

"So, Padre, I tried it and I've liked it so much that I do it a couple of hours every day. I'm careful though. If my daughter saw me talking to an empty chair, she'd either have a nervous breakdown or send me off to the funny farm."

The priest was deeply moved by the story and encouraged the old guy to continue on the journey. Then he prayed with him, anointed him with oil, and returned home.

Two nights later the daughter called to tell the priest that her daddy had died that afternoon.

"Did he seem to die in peace?" he asked.

"Yes, when I left the house around two o'clock, he called me over to his bedside, told me one of his corny jokes, and kissed me on the cheek. When I got back from the store an hour later, I found him dead. But there was something strange, Father. In fact beyond strange, kinda weird. Apparently just before Daddy died, he leaned over and rested his head on a chair beside his bed."

WALKING AROUND LIKE THEY OWN THE JOINT

The Christ of present tense resurrection is as accessible to us as he was to John in his earth suit of human flesh. John knew him first as a physical presence and later in the same way we may know him, as The One we desire above all else. To see Jesus in the flesh was an extraordinary privilege, but read what he said to Thomas, who refused to accept the Resurrection until he saw Jesus alive again and well: "Jesus said, 'So, you believe because you've seen with your own eyes. Even better blessings are in store for those who believe without seeing.'" [13]

The Christ of present tense resurrection is as accessible to us as he was to John in his earth suit of human flesh.

Leadership in the Church of the Present Tense Resurrection is not entrusted to successful fund-raisers, brilliant Bible scholars, administrative geniuses, or spellbinding preachers. Those tools may or may not be in the tool kit of authentic leaders. I fear more often than not that these skills are rewarded because they're so useful in building the sort of structures The Poser appreciates and the Pharisee doesn't hate (and, as we know, the Pharisee seldom has a kind word to say about anything). But I would contend, physical structures of the church aside, the people leading the true growth of the body of Christ are not professionals but those who have been laid waste by a consuming and holy desire for Christ—

passionate men and women for whom recognition and privilege and power mean very little, especially compared to knowing and loving Jesus. Henri Nouwen expounds these qualifications for leadership:

> Christian leaders cannot simply be persons who have well-informed opinions about the burning issues of our time. Their leadership must be rooted in the permanent, intimate relationship with the incarnate Word, Jesus, and they need to find there the source for their words, advice, and guidance. . . . Dealing with burning issues easily leads to divisiveness because, before we know it, our sense of self is caught up in our opinion about a given subject. But when we are securely rooted in personal intimacy with the source of life, it will be possible to remain flexible but not relativistic, convinced without being rigid, willing to confront without being offensive, gentle, and forgiving without being soft, and true witnesses without being manipulative.[14]

All you have to do is look at the places where the historic church bottomed out — those awful spark-flinging periods of hate and abuse and aggression — to find where church leaders were driven by lust and not holy desire. And how would we recognize it if we saw it again? Look for The Poser and the Pharisee walking around like they own the joint.

JUST ENOUGH TO BUY A TREASURE

When Roslyn and I were courting, I grabbed every opportunity to be with her in New Orleans. After concluding a ten-day retreat in Assisi, Italy, for American and Canadian clergy, I flew back with the group to the Twin Cities, arriving at 3:00 A.M.

Exhausted from jet lag and scheduled to speak in just thirty-six hours in San Francisco, the obvious thing was to fly directly to the Bay Area and rest. Instead I stayed in Minneapolis until 6:00 A.M., caught a flight to New Orleans, and shared a delightful picnic with Roslyn on the shores of Lake Pontchartrain. Then on to San Francisco, where I landed at midnight. The next morning I was bright, alert, and energetic, fired by love's urgent longings. Desire can do that for a fella.

Experience tells us that life is not always lived to such a lyrical beat. The root meaning of *infatuation* comes from the Latin *in-fatuus*, "to make foolish."[15] Excitement and enthusiasm must eventually give way to quiet, thoughtful presence or we flame out. The foolishness of infatuation must weather separation, loneliness, conflict, tension, and patches of boredom, or love cannot endure. If love is to survive, the crazy fascination must mature into authentic intimacy marked by self-sacrifice and communication with the beloved.

If love is to survive, the crazy fascination must mature into authentic intimacy marked by self-sacrifice and communication with the beloved.

Many of us can recall an utterly unpredictable moment in which we were deeply touched by an encounter with Jesus Christ. We were swept up in wonder and love. Quite simply, we were infatuated with Jesus, in love with being loved. For me the experience lasted nine years.

Then shortly after ordination I got carried away by success. Applause smothered the heartbeat of God. I was in demand. What a giddy feeling to be admired and sought after! As my unconditional availability to whoever called increased, my intimacy with Christ decreased. I rationalized that this was probably just the price to be paid for unselfish service to the kingdom of God—a little trick I learned from The Poser.

Years later, the fame faded and my popularity waned. When rejection and failure made their first appearance, I was unprepared for the inner devastation. Loneliness and sadness invaded my soul. In search of a mood-altering experience I unplugged the jug. I was a raging drunk within eighteen months. I abandoned the treasure and ran from holy desire.

Eventually, I went for treatment in Hazelden, Minnesota. As the alcoholic fog lifted, I knew there was only one place to go. I sank down into the center of my soul, grew still, and listened again to the Rabbi's heartbeat.

The years since have not been marked by unbroken awareness of the present tense resurrection of Jesus, and my behavior has not been an unbroken spiral toward holiness. There have been lapses and relapses, fits of annoyance and frustration, periods of high anxiety and low self-esteem. The good news for me is that their hang-time grows progressively shorter.

I don't mean to bleed on you. I just want to say that if you're stuck in the swamp of thinking that God works only through saints and heroes, there's dry ground just ahead. God works through the broken-hearted who know they don't have the courage to go on. God works through the weak who know they don't have the strength to carry on. God works through the poor who know whatever it is, they can't buy it.

God puts a treasure in the path of such people to plow into and uncover as they dig in the dirt, and that treasure becomes their holy desire, their obsession. It becomes the longing that won't go away until they've sold all they have—which isn't much, but turns out to be just about exactly enough to buy a piece of present tense resurrection.

Woe to those who think they are alive, for they will taste death soon enough.

Blessed are those who, with good evidence, think they're dead, for they are just about to come alive.

STAND

People. You can't live with 'em, can't live without 'em. Don't get me wrong. Some of my best friends are people. Still . . .

> *Look at your life and see how you have filled its emptiness with people. As a result they have a stranglehold on you. See how they control your behavior by their approval and disapproval. They hold the power to ease your loneliness with their company, to send your spirits soaring with their praise, to bring you down to the depths with their criticism and rejection. Take a look at yourself spending almost every waking moment of your day placating and pleasing people, whether they are living or dead. You live by their norms, conform to their standards, seek their company, desire their love, dread their ridicule, long for their applause, meekly submit to the guilt they lay upon you; you are terrified to go against the fashion in the way you dress or speak or act or even think.* [1]

What it comes down to, for me at least, is dread. I dread disapproval, isolation, abandonment. I dread those who can take away what I depend on. Sometimes I play the game, not to win, but to not lose. I think that's a sorry way to live.

I dread disapproval, isolation, abandonment. I dread those who can take away what I depend on.

The apostle John tells a story about a man who is blind when Jesus meets him. It's the famous *here's mud in your eye* healing.[2] Trouble ensues because the healing is another of those crimes against the Sabbath Jesus keeps committing. The Pharisees are already on the record: No healing on the Sabbath — we don't do it, so neither should you. (Of course, by that standard, there would be no healing allowed on the other six days either, but that's another story.) "Some of the Pharisees said, 'Obviously, this man can't be from God. He doesn't keep the Sabbath.'"[3] *How many times do we have to say it? No good deeds on the day set aside to think about God!*

Someone in the crowd points out that a guy who doesn't respect the Sabbath can't possibly do such a miraculous sign, so the man probably wasn't blind to begin with. This makes sense to everyone and they interview the man alleged to have been healed, who turns out to be just the least bit surly now that he can see. Not a productive exchange of ideas.

Well, if anyone can sort this thing out, it would be the man's parents, so the authorities send for them:

> *They asked them, "Is this your son, the one you say was born blind? So how is it that he now sees?"*
>
> *His parents said, "We know he is our son, and we know he was born blind. But we don't know how he came to see — haven't a clue about who opened his eyes. Why don't you ask him? He's a grown man and can speak for himself." (His parents were talking like this because they were intimidated by the Jewish leaders, who had already decided that anyone who took a stand that this was the Messiah would be kicked out of the meeting place. That's why his parents said, "Ask him. He's a grown man.")*[4]

Sad. One thing leads to another and before it's done, the guy who got his sight from Jesus is excommunicated by the Pharisees. But, hey, his parents didn't get kicked out, so it's not a total loss.

Intimidation is an old tactic in religious circles—*do it our way or you're out.* It shows up again a few chapters later with John's observation that people didn't believe even after Jesus did all kinds of miracles. But, John says, "a considerable number from the ranks of the leaders did believe. But because of the Pharisees, they didn't come out in the open with it. They were afraid of getting kicked out of the meeting place. When push came to shove they cared more for human approval than for God's glory."[5]

We dread, most of us, the punishment that follows any deviation from the party line. We dread it so much we'll do anything to avoid it. We've avoided it so long we're not even certain it will happen. But better safe than sorry.

Hanging on to the approval of the people in power is radically incompatible with authentic faith. The trouble is, the Pharisees are right there in front of us and it's very easy to tell how they think we're doing.

As I already admitted, my dominant sin has been my cowardly refusal to think, feel, act, respond, and live from my authentic self because I fear rejection. That doesn't mean I don't believe in Jesus. Just that I've let peer pressure set the boundaries of my faith. And it doesn't mean I don't love Jesus. Just that there are moments when I love other things—especially my own glittering image—even more. Which means, because I've set these limits on my faith and love for Jesus, it's just a matter of time until my next betrayal. I'm really no different from the first followers of Jesus. When the religious police showed up, "all the disciples cut and ran."[6]

Actually, I am different. The guys who showed up to arrest Jesus did, in fact, arrest and then kill him. The religious police in my world are Christian gurus and people who can invite—or un-invite—me to speak at their events. They are Christian radio personalities, they are lords of commerce; they are my peers. Does that seem odd to you? A guy my age worried about peer pressure?

The tyranny of my peers drives the choices I make and the ones I refuse to make.

I edit myself when I try to predict how the Pharisees will react to my words. So I'm often wishy-washy. No one is much offended because I haven't really taken a stand—I haven't really said anything at all. The tyranny of my peers drives the choices I make and the ones I refuse to make. I'm simply afraid of what people will say. Peter G. van Breeman identified this fear:

> *This fear of ridicule paralyzes more effectively than would a head-on attack or an outspoken harsh criticism. How much good is left undone because of our fear of the opinion of others! We are immobilized by the thought: what will others say? The irony of all this is that the opinions we fear most are not those of people we really respect, yet these same persons influence our lives more than we want to admit. This enervating fear of our peers can create an appalling mediocrity.*[7]

GREAT AND LONELY

When a person finally accepts the profound mystery that she is totally loved by God and there's nothing she can do about that, then she has a fighting chance at embracing her core identity as Abba's Child. And *then* she slowly gains emancipation from all those controlling relationships. She shifts what psychologist Julian Rotter called the *locus of control*—the place where decisions about change are made—from external control to internal self-control. I suppose some people accomplish that shift, more or less, by changing their minds, though I never had much luck at that myself. The person who concentrates on present tense resurrection changes from external to internal control because that's the natural fruit of the Spirit who lives in her: "But the fruit of the Spirit is . . . self-control."[8]

This approach/avoidance thing most of us have with approval never entirely disappears. I still like affirmation when I can get it, but I'm no longer willing to sell my soul—and abandon my holy desire—for a round of applause.

Holy desire is sustainable, not so much as a state of high emotion, but as love's steely determination to do whatever it takes, for as long as it takes, to possess the treasure. That means staying centered in the present tense resurrection of Jesus; it means remaining rooted in the truth of who I am as Abba's totally loved child; it means paying the price of faithfulness.

It's not just about *believing*. As the book of James has it:

> *Do I hear you professing to believe in the one and only God, but then observe you complacently sitting back as if you had done something wonderful? That's just great. Demons do that, but what good does it do them? Use your heads! Do you suppose for a minute that you can cut faith and works in two and not end up with a corpse on your hands?*[9]

A February 2003 Harris Poll uncovered interesting patterns of belief. This is what your friends and neighbors believe in:

> *God:* 90 *percent*
> *Miracles:* 89 *percent*
> *Survival of the soul after death:* 84 *percent*
> *Resurrection of Christ:* 80 *percent*
> *Virgin birth:* 77 *percent*
> *Devil:* 68 *percent*
> *Hell:* 69 *percent*
> *Ghosts:* 51 *percent*
> *Astrology:* 31 *percent*
> *Reincarnation:* 27 *percent*[10]

Does that surprise you? That 89 percent of your neighbors say they believe in miracles? That 80 percent say they believe in the resurrection of Christ? Eighty percent! Do you see evidence of that?

Apparently, *believing* in the Resurrection is not the same as consciously remembering the present tense resurrection of Jesus. One creates self-satisfaction, the other a holy desire that won't quit. The truth of faith has little value when it is not also the life of the heart. Thirteenth-century theologian Anthony of Padua opened every class he taught with the phrase, "Of what value is learning that does not turn to love?"

The truth of faith has little value when it is not also the life of the heart.

The philosopher Sören Kierkegaard mocked the pursuit of biblical and theological knowledge as an end in itself:

We artful dodgers act as if we do not understand the New Testament, because we realize full well that we should have to change our way of life drastically. That is why we invented "religious education" and "christian doctrine." Another concordance, another lexicon, a few more commentaries, three other translations, because it is all so difficult to understand. Yes, of course, dear God, all of us—capitalists, officials, ministers, house-owners, beggars, the whole society—we would be lost if it were not for "scholarly doctrine!"[11]

The one holy desire in Jesus' life was his Father. He carried a secret in his heart that made him great and lonely.[12] The four evangelists do not spare us the brutal details of the losses Jesus suffered to claim his treasure. His family thought he was a little nuts (see Mark 3:21), the Pharisees called him a glutton and a drunkard (see Luke 7:34), the religious scholars spread rumors that he was possessed by the Devil (see Mark 3:22). He was abandoned by those he loved, betrayed by those he trusted, murdered by those he came to rescue. All this he was willing to endure because the treasure is so great.

OUR OWN TWO FEET

The pressure for religious conformity and theological correctness in Christian circles drops us face-to-face in front of what Johannes Metz called "the poverty of uniqueness." Christian folk can make life tough on people who don't color inside the lines. Trusting the way God reveals himself in the Bible has become less important to a lot of people than agreeing with the theology of whatever Christian tribe they call home. "That's all well and good," a deacon responded as the pastor wrapped up a Bible study on racism with his congregational leaders, "but what do we as Baptists believe?"[13]

The poverty of uniqueness may be the price we pay for the treasure we desire. Following Jesus may mean standing utterly alone when the only alternative is selling out our integrity. It may be tenaciously acting like Abba's Child instead of what The Poser thinks we should be or what the Pharisee wants to make us. It may mean trusting Jesus enough to risk making mistakes and asking for do-overs instead of playing it safe.

Following Jesus may mean standing utterly alone when the only alternative is selling out our integrity.

On the desk in the study where I write there's a picture of Thomas Merton with this inscription:

> *If you forget everything else that has been said, I would suggest you remember this for the future: From now on, everybody stands on his own two feet.*

Standing on our own two feet is an often heroic act of love for God and those he asks us to serve—no matter what The Poser says or how the Pharisee criticizes—whatever the cost; however long it takes; alone if necessary.

The only kind of uniqueness The Poser understands is signified by *best, most, finest, first*—things that can be turned into newspaper articles or job offers. The Poser is horrified and baffled by qualifiers like *least, last,* and *lost*. He wonders why in the world anyone would do that to themselves? If we can't be best or first, The Poser's advice is "Lie low, stay under the radar, don't make waves, say what everyone else is saying and do what they're doing; don't stand up if you can't stand out."

The real measure of our deep awareness of Christ's present tense resurrection is our capacity to stand up for the truth when it attracts disapproval from people who are important to us. A deep and holy desire for truth musters a growing indifference to public opinion, whatever people think or say. The safety of drifting with the crowd and echoing the opinions of others begins to feel not just false, but terribly dull.

When we learn to hear it, the inner voice that whispers, "Take courage. Don't be afraid. It's me," tells us our security rests in having no security. When a person stands on her own two feet and claims responsibility for her unique self—when the only opinion that matters is the opinion of her Abba—she finds herself growing in freedom, fortitude, and liberation from the bondage of human approval.

YOU CAN'T FAKE THAT

Psychology and religion both place strong emphasis on the priority of *being* over *doing*. We are often reminded by pastors, therapists, and next-door neighbors, "It is not what you *do* that matters, it is who you *are*." And of course they're right. At least partly right.

I have a friend who called himself a writer for a long time before he actually wrote anything. Which is to say he liked the sound of his voice saying, "I'm a writer." But he didn't particularly want to write anything because writing—as anyone who's tried it can tell you—is difficult. "Easy reading is damn hard writing," Nathaniel Hawthorne is supposed to have said. Not hard like picking fruit all day, hard like taking a test all day.

After stumbling over the question, "Oh really? What do you write?" my friend discovered that the evidence of *being* is *doing*.

This is one of the dilemmas the book of James wrestles with, and it's one reason quite a few theologians and thinkers (including Martin Luther) never cared much for James. "Use your heads!" James says. "Do you suppose for a minute that you can cut faith and works in two and not end up with a corpse on your hands?"[14] Luther wrote, "He wishes to guard against those who depended on faith without going on to works, but he had neither the spirit, nor the thought, nor the eloquence equal to the task." Luther's solution was to refuse James "a place among the writers of the true canon" in his Bible.[15] Not one of Luther's best moments.

This faith and works thing is one of those difficulties people like to smooth over. But it's not easily smoothed. Our identity as Abba's totally loved child is the truest thing about us. Our behavior as Abba's totally loved child authenticates that identity.

Now can't you just hear the Pharisee gloating, *I told you it was all about the doing, and doing is about the Law, and I know more about the Law than anyone, so I win!*

I think we've already covered that. Constructing a self-image based on religious acts leads to the illusion of self-righteousness. When our sense of self is tied to any particular task—from serving in a soup kitchen to promoting a biblical environmental consciousness, to preaching and teaching—working, not love, becomes our core value; we lose touch with our true self and the happy combination of mysterious dignity and pompous dust which we really are.

And yet . . .

What we do in Christ may express the ultimate truth of who we are in Christ more than anything else.

I want to affirm that what we *do* in Christ may express the ultimate truth of who we *are* in Christ more than anything else. I'm not suggesting stockpiling frequent righteousness points to earn a flight to heaven. But who we are is elusive. I'm suggesting what I think Frederick Buechner was getting at when he wrote,

> *Introspection in the long run doesn't get you very far because every time you draw back to look at yourself, you are seeing everything except for the part that drew back, and when you draw back to look at the part that drew back to look at yourself, you see again everything except for what you are really looking for. And so on. Since the possibilities for drawing back seem to be infinite, you are, in your quest to see yourself whole, doomed always to see infinitely less than what there will always remain to see. Thus, when you wake up in the morning, called by God to be a self again, if you want to know who you are, watch your feet. Because where your feet take you, that is who you are.*[16]

That's what I'm getting at. The Poser fabricates. The Pharisee falsifies. Abba's Child loves until he gets it right.

You can't fake that, not for long.

Simon Tugwell wrote,

> *What we do can be much more versatile and worthwhile than what goes on behind the scenes of our psychological life. And it may be of greater significance for our being in God, because it*

may express his true purpose, even while it does not express
anything we could clearly call our own purpose.[17]

Paul addresses the issue like this: "God can do anything, you know—
far more than you could ever imagine or guess or request in your
wildest dreams! He does it not by pushing us around but by working
within us, his Spirit deeply and gently within us."[18]

WWGD?

The Christian commitment is not a vague concept that means whatever
we want it to mean. It is a concrete, visible, courageous, awe-inspiring
way of being in the world. It's forged by daily choices to pursue our
holy desire to live in the present tense resurrection. A commitment
that's not gradually evident in the form of humble service, compassionate discipleship, and creative love is an illusion. And we know what
Jesus thinks about illusions: "If you just use my words in Bible studies
and don't work them into your life, you are like a stupid carpenter who
built his house on the sandy beach. When a storm rolled in and the
waves came up, it collapsed like a house of cards" (Matthew 7:26-27).
Too bad about that house down on the beach. It had a great view while
it lasted.

Maybe one reason the spokesmodels of Christian theology seem to
know only one song—the one about personal salvation—is that they
are less sure about what Jesus meant than, say, your above average man
of Hindu descent. Gandhi was perfectly clear about the difference
between Christianity and Christ. Try this on for size:

When I began as a prayerful student to study Christian liter-
ature in South Africa in 1893, I asked myself again and again,

*"Is this Christianity?" And I could only say, "No, no.
Certainly this that I see is not Christianity." And the deepest in
me tells me that I was right; for it was unworthy of Jesus and
untrue to the Sermon on the Mount.*[19]

Or this:

*Europe does not believe in [the New Testament]. . . . They do
claim to respect it, although only a few know and observe
Christ's religion of peace.*[20]

Or this:

*If, then, I had to face only the Sermon on the Mount and my
own interpretation of it, I should not hesitate to say, "Oh yes,
I am a Christian." But I know that at the present moment if I
said any such thing I would lay myself open to the gravest mis-
interpretation.*

*But negatively I can tell you that to my mind much of that
which passes for Christianity is a negation of the Sermon on the
Mount. Please mark my words carefully. I am not at the present moment speaking especially of Christian conduct; I am
speaking of Christian belief, of Christianity as it is understood
in the West.*[21]

Gandhi was willing to let us off the hook for failure to live up to the
high calling of Christian faith. But, based on what he saw Christians do
in the world, his unfortunate conclusion was that we don't even *believe*
the right stuff. If you think he was completely wrong about that, read

the Sermon on the Mount and compare it with the way Christian people regard our enemies. We're going to have to step up to the plate on this. Or be prepared to endure a rash of "What Would Gandhi Do?" bracelets.[22]

LISTEN TO MY HEARTBEAT

The stark realism of the Bible's portrait of Christ leaves no room for romanticized idealism or sloppy sentimentality. The night before his execution, Jesus washed his disciples' feet.

> Then he said, "Do you understand what I have done to you? You address me as 'Teacher' and 'Master,' and rightly so. That is what I am. So if I, the Master and Teacher, washed your feet, you must now wash each other's feet. I've laid down a pattern for you. What I've done, you do. I'm only pointing out the obvious. A servant is not ranked above his master; an employee doesn't give orders to the employer. If you understand what I'm telling you, act like it—and live a blessed life."[23]

Servanthood is not an emotion or mood or feeling; it's a decision to live like Jesus even when we don't feel like it.

Servanthood is not an emotion or mood or feeling; it's a decision to live like Jesus even when we don't feel like it. A few hours after this foot-washing episode, Jesus wasn't feeling much like sacrificing his life for humankind: "Going a little ahead, he fell on his face, praying, "My Father, if there is any way, get me out of this. But please, not what I want. You, what do *you* want?"[24] Jesus found the source for obeying his Abba *in his Abba*, not in his own emotional reserves. That's a much better ending than *I was going to save the world . . . but then I didn't feel like it.* Thank God, Jesus was who he was and did what the Father asked him to do. God help us do the same.

When *being* is divorced from *doing*, pious thoughts become an adequate substitute for washing dirty feet. The call to the servant life of Jesus is a call away from the secular standard of human greatness and to a life of holy desire for something that never fades away. As we participate in the foot-washing experience, Jesus addresses us directly as he looks into our eyes and makes this fantastic claim: *If you want to know what God is like, look at me. If you want to learn that your God does not come to rule but to redeem, watch me. If you want assurance that you did not invent the story of God's love, rest your head on my chest and listen to my heartbeat.*

THE DOG'S DILEMMA

A dog of average (which is to say almost no) intelligence lies in the dirt, gnawing a bone. The bone, once a vital part of some cow's structural integrity, is now depleted of marrow and moisture, worthless for anything beyond stimulating the canine's gums and exercising his jaws.

You approach the dog, hands behind your back; he eyes you, suspicious. You speak kindly; he wags his tail slowly, smiles a doggy smile, and places a paw on top of the bone, sniffing the air uncertainly.

After a moment, he returns to the bone with a lick, and is about to resume gnawing when you bring your hands from behind your back, revealing half a pound of fresh ground beef. This maneuver captures the dog's attention and he wags his tail appreciatively while covering the bone again with his paw. You have to pay respects to a human with fresh beef—he knows this but can't remember why.

You smile and straighten your arm a bit—the one with the meat piled on the end of it. The dog smiles back and licks his lips. You take half a tentative step forward, extending the meat as if to offer it to the dog and he, after a moment of frozen indecision, stands to his feet and picks up the bone, never taking his eyes off you.

You take another half step forward. Nothing has changed, you're still smiling, still offering the burger, and you would think, because he is your dog, who sneaks into your bed after you fall asleep, who licks fried chicken grease right off your hand and drinks from your open toilet—you would think the beast would see your approach as nothing if not promising. But incredibly, he backs away, his eyes mapping out an escape route lest he become cornered and you do something terrible.

This is not your intention at all. You seek only his good and offer half a pound of lean ground chuck as proof. And so what if there is the tiniest bit of doggy medicine mixed with the beef—that too is for his good, and you expect if he knows anything at all he would know this.

And to be fair, he suspects it in a vague, dreamy way—you are the one who goes away and then comes back so marvelously, and he has no idea how you do that but he is mightily impressed every time. And you are the one who appears on occasion with food or a ball or a piece of whadaya-call-it . . . rope! And what great fun that is until his gums bleed and you pin him to the floor and say "No more!" so sternly. He's not sure why you have to be so strict, but he loves you and gets excited when he hears the noise that means you'll come through that wall opening that appears and then disappears so suddenly—and how in the world does that work? he wonders. And now here you are with meat! You have meat, and boy does that look good, and his nostrils flare as you wave that tasty treat in front of him, and he doesn't really know why he's backing up with that nasty bone when you're right there with a huge chunk of fresh beef and all he has to do — he knows this somehow as his tail drops, still wagging between his hind legs — all he has to do is let go of the bone. Just drop the bone and you'll almost certainly — he doesn't know why you would, but it's not his to question; he hasn't, as far as he can remember, done anything to deserve it, but you're so good that way; it's part of why he loves you — you will almost certainly give him the meat, and all he has to do is drop the bone, and golly does that meat look good, and boy is this bone ever dry, and he would, he would take the meat in a second because he trusts you and believes in you and you're holding meat right out in front of him almost touching his nose. And his tail is between his legs and hardly even wagging anymore — it's just one too many operations under the circumstances — and the circumstances are that you have the beef, and he's pretty doggone sure you'll give it to him if he'll just drop the bone, but you gotta understand, the beef is just a promise, and he knows it may not be much but he's *got* the bone.

That's the dog's dilemma. You see his problem don't you?[25]

The Poser, well-intentioned liar, is nothing if not consistent. *Work that bone like it was the best thing you ever tasted. Sell it! You can make them believe if you sell it; they want to believe; just give them what they want and they'll give you what you want. Look, I took the liberty of hiring a skin consultant and a publicist. I'm not sure we're making the most out of the whole crime-to-Christ angle. Hey, I don't suppose you've ever actually been in prison have you? Because that would make a book right there, maybe a series. I have to tell you, I'm very excited about this, very excited.*

The Pharisee, stern ambassador from the master race, has nothing but contempt for you and your kind. *Tear it down and start over. You're hopeless. I don't know why you bother. Okay, listen: I'll go over this one more time. You show up for the formation every time, on time, and prepared. Dress like me, talk like me, eat what I eat and only what I eat. There will be no excursions outside the compound and no fraternizing with the enemy. Any questions? I didn't think so. Now take this telephone cord, go to your room, and beat yourself to sleep. And don't forget your bone!*

///

None of this has anything to do with the present tense resurrection of Jesus. None of this has anything to do with holy desire. None of this has anything to do with the Rabbi's heartbeat. None of this has anything whatsoever to do with being Abba's Child. So whatever it is, however long you've been sucking on it, it's dead now, it will never get any tastier or more nutritious than it is right now. So come on, drop the bone, take the meat. There's more where that comes from.

The apostle Paul gets the last word:

> *Be prepared. You're up against far more than you can handle on your own. Take all the help you can get, every weapon God has issued, so that when it's all over but the shouting you'll still be on your feet.*[26]

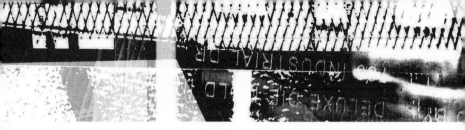

NOTES

CHAPTER ONE: COME OUT, COME OUT, WHEREVER YOU ARE

1. Flannery O'Connor, *The Collected Works of Flannery O'Connor* (New York: Farrar, Strauss, Giroux, 1991), pp. 42-54.
2. A. W. Tozer, *The Knowledge of the Holy* (New York: Harper & Row, 1961), p. 9.
3. Julian of Norwich, *The Revelations of Divine Love* (New York: Penguin, 1966), chap. 73.
4. Anne Lamott, *Operating Instructions* (New York: Pantheon, 1993), p. 96.
5. 1 John 4:18.
6. Julian of Norwich, chap. 39.
7. Simon Tugwell, *The Beatitudes: Soundings in Christian Tradition* (Springfield, Ill.: Templegate Publishers, 1980), p. 130.
8. Thomas Merton, *The Hidden Ground of Love: Letters* (New York: Farrar, Strauss, Giroux, 1985), p. 38.
9. David Seamands, *Healing for Damaged Emotions* (Wheaton, Ill.: Victor, 1981), p. 49.
10. Morton Kelsey, *Encounters with God*, quoted by Parker Palmer, in "The Monastic Renewal of the Church," Desert Call (Crestone, Colo.).
11. Henri J. M. Nouwen, *Life of the Beloved* (New York: Crossroad, 1992), p. 21.
12. *Postcards from the Edge*, Columbia Pictures, 1990.
13. Matthew 5:4.
14. James Finley, *Merton's Palace of Nowhere* (Notre Dame, Ind.: Ave Maria Press, 1978), p. 53.
15. 2 Corinthians 12:10.
16. Thornton Wilder, *The Angel That Troubled the Waters and Other Plays* (New York: Coward-McCann, 1928), p. 20.
17. Don Finto in "Old Friend," *Real Kids: Survivors: Powerful Profiles on Addiction, Violence, & Loss*, Youth Specialties video.
18. James A. Knight, M.D., *Psychiatry and Religion: Overlapping Concerns*, Lillian Robinson, M.D., ed. (Washington, DC: American Psychiatric Press, 1986). Knight's splendid article, "The Religio-Psychological Dimension of Wounded Healers" is the principal source of my reflections here. My gratitude to him and Lillian Robinson for introducing me to the book.

CHAPTER TWO: THE POSER

1. *Zelig*, Warner Bros., 1983.
2. James Masterson, *The Search for the Real Self* (New York: Free Press, 1988), p. 67.
3. John Bradshaw, *Home Coming* (New York/Toronto: Bantam Books, 1990), p. 8.
4. 1 John 1:8.
5. Susan Howatch, *Glittering Images* (New York: Ballantine Books, 1987), p. 278.
6. Thomas Merton, quoted by James Finley, *Merton's Palace of Nowhere* (Notre Dame, Ind.: Ave Maria Press, 1978), p. 34.
7. 2 Corinthians 5:14-16.
8. Howatch, p. 162.
9. Masterson, p. 65.
10. Jeffrey D. Imbach, *The Recovery of Love* (New York: Crossroad, 1992), pp. 62-63.
11. Finley, p. 36.
12. Thomas Merton, *New Seeds of Contemplation* (New York: New Directions, 1961), p. 35.
13. Annie Dillard, *Teaching a Stone to Talk* (New York: HarperPerennial, 1982), p. 49.
14. Philomena Agudo, *Intimacy, the Third Psychotheological Symposium* (Whitinsville, Mass.: Affirmation Books, 1978), p. 21.
15. C. J. Jung, *Modern Man in Search of a Soul* (New York: Harcourt, Brace and World Harvest Books, 1933), p. 235.

CHAPTER THREE: WHO'S YOUR DADDY?

1. William Least Heat Moon, *Blue Highways* (New York: Fawcett Crest, 1982), pp. 108-109.
2. Monica Furlong, *Merton: A Biography* (San Francisco, Calif.: Harper and Row, 1980), p. 18.
3. John Eagan, *A Traveler Toward the Dawn* (Chicago: Loyola University Press, 1990).
4. Thomas Merton, quoted by James Finley, *Merton's Palace of Nowhere* (Notre Dame, Ind.: Ave Maria Press, 1978), p. 71.
5. Eagan, pp. 150-151.
6. Henri J. M. Nouwen, *Life of the Beloved* (New York: Crossroad, 1992), p. 26.
7. Finley, p. 96.
8. Michael Yaconelli, *The Door Magazine*.
9. Edward Schillebeeckx, *The Church and Mankind* (New York: Seabury Press, 1976), p. 118.
10. Frederick Buechner, *The Clown in the Belfry* (San Francisco, Calif.: Harper, 1992), p. 171.

CHAPTER FOUR: ABBA'S CHILD

1. You can learn more about this from Joachim Jeremias, *The Parables of Jesus* (New York: Charles Scribner, 1970), especially p. 128.

2. John 19:7.

3. Romans 8:14-16.

4. 1 John 3:1-2.

5. Matthew 11:27.

6. Gerald G. May, *Addiction and Grace* (San Francisco, Calif.: Harper and Row, 1988), p. 168.

7. Luke 1:78-79.

8. Isaiah 49:15.

9. Richard J. Foster, Prayer, *Finding the Heart's True Home* (San Francisco, Calif.: Harper, 1992), p. 85.

10. Hans Kung, *On Being a Christian* (New York: Doubleday, 1976), p. 32.

11. Kung, p. 33.

12. 1 John 3:1-3.

13. Donald Gray, *Jesus — The Way to Freedom* (Winona, Minn.: St. Mary's College Press, 1979), p. 70.

14. Matthew 18:21-35.

15. Stephen Covey, *The Seven Habits of Highly Effective People*, Audiocassette Seminar (Provo, Utah).

16. Franklin Graham in his opening address to Prescription for Hope, the International Christian Conference on HIV/AIDS, 17 February 2002.

17. Mark Ross with Lindy Warren in the Gospel Music Association's *GMAil*, 3 July 2002.

18. Sheryl Henderson Blunt in *Christianity Today*, 22 April 2002, vol. 46, no. 5, p. 18.

19. Bono to Canadian Broadcasting Company's Peter Mansbridge, on CBC TV's *The National*, 28 June 2002.

20. Calle Almedal to Timothy C. Morgan in *Christianity Today*, 22 April 2002, vol. 46, no. 5, p. 5.

21. Bono to St. Paul's United Methodist Church, Chicago, *Chicago Tribune*, 3 December 2002.

22. 1 Corinthians 4:5, author paraphrase.

23. Alan Jones, *Exploring Spiritual Direction* (Minneapolis, Minn.: Winston Press, 1982), p. 17. This book and another by Jones, *Soul Making, The Desert Way of Spirituality* (Harper and Row, 1985), have been a source of deep insight and endless meditation for me.

24. Henri J. M. Nouwen, *Life of the Beloved* (New York: Crossroad, 1992), p. 34.

25. Robert J. Wicks, *Touching the Holy* (Notre Dame, Ind.: Ave Maria Press, 1992), p. 87.

26. Adapted from Wendell Berry, *The Hidden Wound* (San Francisco, Calif.: North Point Press, 1989), p. 4. I appropriated Berry's thoughts and words on his struggle with racism and expanded them to include homosexuality.

27. Frederick Buechner, *The Clown in the Belfry* (San Francisco, Calif.: Harper, 1992), p. 146.

28. Luke 10:36-37.

29. Anthony DeMello, *The Way to Love* (New York: Doubleday, 1991), p. 77.

CHAPTER FIVE: HOLIER THAN GOD

1. Philosopher Bertrand Russell, *Why I Am Not a Christian, and Other Essays on Religion and Related Subjects* (New York: Simon and Schuster, 1957), p. 35.

2. Genesis 1:31–2:3.

3. See Exodus 16.

4. Exodus 20:8-11.

5. Exodus 31:12-15.

6. Isaiah 58:13-14.

7. The tradition stuck. In Luke 7, we find Jesus, the traveling preacher, having dinner on the Sabbath in the home of Simon the Pharisee.

8. You can read that story beginning in 2 Kings 24.

9. T. S. Eliot, *Murder in the Cathedral*, part 1.

10. Matthew 12:1-8.

11. Matthew 12:9-16.

12. Eugene Kennedy, *The Choice to Be Human* (New York: Doubleday, 1985), p. 128.

13. 1 John 4:19.

14. Kennedy, p. 211.

15. Thomas Merton, quoted by James Finley, *Merton's Palace of Nowhere* (Notre Dame, Ind.: Ave Maria Press, 1978), p. 54.

16. Matthew 23:23-28.

17. Luke 18:11-12.

18. In Simon Tugwell, *The Beatitudes: Soundings in Christian Traditions* (Springfield, Ill.: Templegate Publishers, 1980), p. 138.

19. Brennan Manning, *A Stranger to Self-Hatred* (Denville, N.J.: Dimension Books, 1982), p. 97.

20. Luke 7:11-15.

21. Anthony DeMello, *Awareness: A Spirituality Conference in His Own Words* (New York: Doubleday, 1990), p. 28.

22. Matthew 18:1-4.

23. John Shea, *Starlight* (New York: Crossroad, 1993), p. 92.

24. DeMello, *The Way to Love*, (Image Books, 1995), p. 73.

25. Quoted by DeMello, *The Way to Love*, p. 76.

26. Ernest Hemingway, *A Farewell to Arms* (New York: Scribner's and Sons, 1957), p. 249.

27. William McNamara, *Mystical Passion* (Amity, N.Y.: Amity House, 1977), p. 57.

28. Jeffrey D. Imbach, *The Recovery of Love* (New York: Crossroad, 1992), p. 103.

29. Jean Gill, *Unless You Become Like a Child* (New York: Paulist Press, 1985), p. 39.

30. Anne Tyler, *Saint Maybe* (New York: Simon & Schuster, 1982), p. 124.

31. Frederick Buechner, *The Magnificent Defeat* (San Francisco, Calif.: Harper and Row, 1966), p. 135.

CHAPTER SIX: RESURRECTION

1. 1 Corinthians 15:3-4.

2. Philippians 3:8-11.

3. C. S. Lewis, *Letters to an American Lady*, edited by Clide Kilby (Grand Rapids, Mich.: Eerdmans), p. 84.

4. H. A. Williams, *True Resurrection* (London: Mitchell Begley Limited, 1972), p. 5.

5. Hebrews 7:25.

6. Matthew 28:18-20.

7. William Barry, *God's Passionate Desire and Our Response* (Notre Dame, Ind.: Ave Maria Press, 1993), p. 109.

8. "A Conversation with Frederick Buechner," *Image: A Journal of the Arts and Religion*, Spring 1989, pp. 56-57.

9. Brennan Manning, *The Ragamuffin Gospel* (Portland, Ore.: Multnomah, 1990), p. 89.

10. John 7:37-39.

11. John 14:15-17.

12. John 14:25-26.

13. John 15:26-27.

14. John 16:4-15.

15. Acts 1:4-8.

16. Acts 2:1-11.

17. Colossians 1:27.

18. Barry, p. 87. In a chapter titled "Mysticism in Hell" Barry relates the astonishing story of the Dutch Jewess who journaled her conviction that God was not absent in the concentration camp.

19. Anne Tyler, *Saint Maybe* (New York: Simon & Schuster, 1982), pp. 199-200.

20. Romans 8:26-28.

21. John 14:1-9.

22. C. S. Lewis, *Mere Christianity* (New York: Collier/MacMillan, 1952), p. 47.

23. Barry, p. 115.

24. Matthew 9:36.

25. Isaiah 40:11.

26. John McKenzie, *Source: What the Bible Says About the Problems of Contemporary Life* (Chicago: Thomas More Press, 1984), p. 206.

27. John 15:5.

28. Peter G. van Breeman, *Called by Name* (Denville, N.J.: Dimension Books, 1976), p. 38.

29. Richard Schickel, "More Than a Heart Warmer: Frank Capra: 1897-1991," *Time* magazine, 138, 16 September 1991, no. 11, p. 77. Extracted by Walter Burghardt, *When Christ Meets Christ* (Mahwah, N.J.: Paulist Press, 1993), p. 77.

30. M. Scott Peck, *The Road Less Traveled* (Touchstone, 2003).

CHAPTER SEVEN: HOLY DESIRE

1. C. S. Lewis, *The Weight of Glory and Other Addresses* (New York: Macmillan, revised and expanded, 1980), pp. 3-4.

2. Much embellished from Matthew 13:44.

3. Matthew 13:44.

4. Jeffrey D. Imbach, *The Recovery of Love* (New York: Crossroad, 1992), p. 134.

5. Adapted from John Shea, *Starlight* (New York: Crossroad, 1993), pp. 115-117. This story, courtesy of Reuben Gold and the Hasidic tradition, was drastically reworked by Shea, whose early works, *Stories of Faith* and *Stories of God*, are a treasure trove of modern parables coupled with a brilliant analysis of the power of storytelling.

6. Matthew 5:8.

7. Jeremiah 31:33-34.

8. See John 13:23,25.

9. 1 John 4:18.

10. In Robert J. Wicks, *Touching the Holy* (Notre Dame, Ind.: Ave Maria Press, 1992), p. 14.

11. John 21:20, NIV.

12. Brennan Manning, *Lion and Lamb: The Relentless Tenderness of Jesus* (Old Tappan, N.J.: Revell/Chosen, 1986), pp. 129-130. Now available through Baker Book House (Grand Rapids, Mich.). Quoting from one's own previously published works is a desperate measure but sales are slipping and I need a pair of sandals.

13. John 20:29.

14. Henri J. M. Nouwen, *In the Name of Jesus* (New York: Crossroad, 1989), p. 42.

15. Thomas J. Tyrell, *Urgent Longings: Reflections on the Experience of Infatuation, Human Intimacy, and Contemplative Love* (Whitinsville, Mass.: Affirmation Books, 1980), p. 17.

CHAPTER EIGHT: STAND

1. Anthony DeMello, *The Way to Love* (New York: Doubleday, 1991), p. 64.

2. It's a good read: John chapter 9.

3. John 9:16.

4. John 9:18-23.

5. John 12:42-43.

6. Matthew 26:56.

7. Peter G. van Breeman, *Called By Name* (Denville, N.J.: Dimension Books, 1976), p. 88.

8. Galatians 5:22-23, NIV.

9. James 2:19-20.

10. *The Harris Poll* no. 11, 26 February 2003. ISSN 0895-7983. http://www.harrisinteractive.com/harris_poll/index.asp?PID=359

11. In Peter G. van Breeman, *Called By Name* (Denville, N.J.: Dimension Books, 1976), p. 39.

12. For more on this idea, see Johannes B. Metz, *Poverty of Spirit* (New York/Mahwah, N.J.: Paulist Press, 1968), pp. 39-40.

13. From a sermon by Robert McMillan, First Baptist Church, Tallahassee, Florida.

14. James 2:20.

15. Martin Luther, Preface to the Epistles of St. James and St. Jude, quoted by William Barclay, *The Letters of James and Peter* (Philadelphia: Westminster Press, 1976), pp. 7-8.

16. Frederick Buechner, *The Alphabet of Grace* (New York: Harper & Row, 1970), pp. 24-25.

17. Simon Tugwell, *The Beatitudes: Soundings in Christian Traditions* (Springfield, Ill.: Templegate Publishers, 1980), pp. 54-55.

18. Ephesians 3:20.

19. Mahatma Gandhi in C. F. Andrews, *Mahatma Gandhi's Ideas: Including Selections from His Writings* (London: The Macmillan Company, 1930), p. 95.

20. Mahatma Gandhi in *Rashmi-SudhaPuri, Gandhi on War and Peace* (New York: Praeger Publishers, 1987), p. 17.

21. Andrews, p. 94.

22. You'll find the Sermon on the Mount in Matthew chapters 5–7.

23. John 13:12-17.

24. Matthew 26:39.

25. Thanks to Bill Reif who did something like The Dog's Dilemma for the high school kids at First Presbyterian Church in Colorado Springs a long, long time ago.

26. Ephesians 6:13.

ABOUT THE AUTHORS

BRENNAN MANNING is a writer and speaker who leads spiritual retreats for people of all ages and backgrounds. He is the author of more than ten books, including *Ruthless Trust*, *The Boy Who Cried Abba*, and *The Ragamuffin Gospel*. A resident of New Orleans, he travels extensively in the U.S. and abroad to share the good news of the unconditional love of God.

JIM HANCOCK worked with adolescents and families for two decades before turning his hand to filmmaking, writing, and speaking to students, youth workers, and parents. He has developed nearly two hundred documentary films for or about kids and he's the author of *Raising Adults*, *Good Sex*, *The Good Sex Dramas*, *The Justice Mission*, *The Compassion Project*, *Dramatic Pauses*, and *The Boy Who Believed in Magic*. Most mornings you'll find Jim writing at The Potato Shack in Encinitas, California.

The Message Remix
Eugene H. Peterson
Hardcover
1-57683-434-4
Bonded Alligator Leather
1-57683-450-6

God's Word was meant to be read and understood. It was first written in the language of the people — of fishermen, shopkeepers, and carpenters. *The Message Remix* gets back to that feel. Plus the new verse-numbered paragraphs make it easier to study.

Promises. Promises. Promises.
Eugene H. Peterson
1-57683-466-2

Everybody's making promises these days.
But who's really true to their word?

God is. Take a look at His promises — promises of a real life and a future. See how knowing them can help you trust God even more.

The Message:
The Gospel of John
in Contemporary Language
Eugene H. Peterson
1-57683-432-8

Read what John witnessed as he walked alongside Jesus. Then help others find hope and a new way of life — better and more real than they've ever dreamed of experiencing. Share it with everyone you know!

Get the Bible off your shelf and into your heart.

Memorize This: TMS 3.0
1-57683-457-3

Why memorize anything? Laptops, cell phones, PDA's do all the memorizing for you, right? Well, not really. When you need something RIGHT NOW, it needs to be stored in your heart.

That's how God's Word should be—so when something happens, it's right there. After all, how did Jesus handle temptation? He quoted God's Word in its face. A specialized version of NavPress' successful *Topical Memory System*, this book will help you deal with whatever life throws at you—if the words are in your heart, and not just in your machines.

Because they don't offer Talking to God 101.
(Even though they should.)

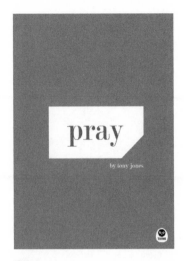

Pray
Tony Jones
1-57683-452-2

Do you ever feel a little stumped about prayer—like you keep saying the same things over and over again? Maybe you don't know how to get started.

With this book, you'll learn by the solid example of those who have gone before us. The prayers of these men and women—the prophets, the apostles, the early and modern church, and even Jesus himself—can help us pray more effectively. Author Tony Jones highlights the important features of these powerful prayers—so you can enjoy talking to God as much as they did.

1-800-366-7788
www.th1nkbooks.com
THINK

Practice your faith. Every day.

Read, Think, Pray, Live
A guide to reading the Bible in a new way
Tony Jones
1-57683-453-0

If you want to know Jesus and what He's all about, try doing these four—read, think, pray, live. It's how your faith can grow. *Lectio divina*, or sacred reading, is a time-tested method used by believers to experience God in a personal and real way.

Tailored for students, this book teaches you how to engage your faith. Learning from a method of contemplative study that has worked for hundreds of years, you'll find yourself challenged and encouraged to get to know God in brand-new ways.

1-800-366-7788
www.th1nkbooks.com

THiNK

Knowing God isn't just a walk—it's a chase.

The Chase
Pursuing Holiness in Your Everyday Life
Jerry Bridges
1-57683-468-9

The Bible calls us to be holy. Is that even possible? There must have been some glitch in the translation, right?

That depends on your definition of holy. If by it you mean "always perfect, never making a mistake" you're right—that's impossible. But if by holy you mean "wanting and doing the right things," that can be done with the aid of the Holy Spirit.

Taken from the NavPress classic *The Pursuit of Holiness*, this book shows students how "running as to get the prize" isn't just possible, it's what life is all about.

Available Fall 2003

1-800-366-7788
www.th1nkbooks.com

What if He were born in Bethlehem . . . Pennsylvania?

!HERO Comics and Graphic Novel
Comic 1: 1-57683-504-9
Comic 2: 1-57683-501-4
Comic 3: 1-57683-502-2
Comic 4: 1-57683-503-0
*Graphic Novel: 1-57683-500-6

*includes comics 1-4 plus the previously unreleased comic 5

Follow the !HERO action up close and personal! Read as Special Agent Alex Hunter strives to discover the story behind a mysterious miracle-worker from Bethlehem, Pennsylvania, whose very presence is changing the world.

In a series of five action-packed episodes, best-selling author Stephen R. Lawhead, collaborating with author and penciler Ross Lawhead, incites the imagination to wonder: What if He were born today? Collect all four comics, then pick up the graphic novel to get issue five!

Check out www.herouniverse.com for more information.

1-800-366-7788
www.th1nkbooks.com